Negotiating Law, Policing and Morality in African: A Handbook for Policing in Zimbabwe

Misheck P. Chingozha & Munyaradzi Mawere

Langaa Research & Publishing CIG
Mankon, Bamenda

Publisher
Langaa RPCIG
Langaa Research & Publishing Common Initiative Group
P.O. Box 902 Mankon
Bamenda
North West Region
Cameroon
Langaagrp@gmail.com
www.langaa-rpcig.net

Distributed in and outside N. America by African Books Collective
orders@africanbookscollective.com
www.africanbookscollective.com

ISBN: 9956-762-05-9

Table of Contents

Table of Contents

Acknowledgements

We owe a debt of gratitude to many people in Mashonaland Central and Masvingo Provinces of Zimbabwe who collaborated and assisted us in many ways too numerous to mention during fieldwork for this book.

Just to single out a few names; we wish to acknowledge our indebtedness to Artwell Nhemachena for providing us with some of the important research materials for this book. Your generosity and steadfast support throughout this project is commendable.

Our profound and honest gratitude also go to Tapuwa R. Mubaya for conscientiously going through this book before it was sent out for publication. Your review was thorough and meticulous that it provided us with some wonderful insights that took our arguments to a higher level.

It will be unfair to leave out Sydney Manonose who took his precious time helping us with the typing of part of the first draft of the manuscript that resulted in this book. Thank you so much for this sincere patience, bounteousness, and the laudable much-needed support you rendered us.

To Yeukai Chingozha and Annastacia Mawere, no words can adequately express our profound gratitude for your overwhelmingly unwavering support and cheering during the time which data for this book was gathered. You always stood with us! We thank you so much for this untiring moral support that boosted not only our confidence but encouraged us to work even harder and faster.

Finally to God, you will not cease to amaze us for faithfully standing with us all the time.

List of Acronyms and Abbreviations

APTS	African Police Training School Depot
AG	Attorney General
BBC	British Broadcasting Corporation
BSAP	British South Africa Police
CID	Criminal Investigation Department
CGP	Commissioner General of Police
CMP	Commissioner of Metropolitan Police
CLEAJ	Commission on Law Enforcement and Administration of Justice
CJRC	Criminal Justice Resource Centre
CPC	Central Planning Committee
CRLO	Community Relations Liaison Officer
GMO	Governmental Medical Officer
ICPC	Independent Corruption Practices Corruption
LEAP	Legal Education Action Project
MDG	Millennium Development Goal
NGO	Non-governmental Organisation
NS	Native Sergeant
NWC	Neighbourhood Watch Committee
PATU	Police Anti-Terrorist Unit
PHQ	Police Headquarters
SAP	South African Police
UDHR	Universal Declaration of Human Rights
UNHRC	United Nations Human Rights Charter
UN	United Nations
TKK	Toa Kitu Kidogo
ZANLA	Zimbabwe African National Liberation Army
ZBC	Zimbabwe Broadcasting Corporation
ZIPRA	Zimbabwe People's Revolutionary Army
ZG	Zimbabwe Government
ZRP	Zimbabwe Republic Police

Chapter One

Law, Policing, and Morality: An Introduction

Introduction

This book derives from a concern of the authors with the contemporary criminal justice especially policing in Africa, and particularly Zimbabwe. Although the book focuses on criminal justice in contemporary Zimbabwe, it draws examples from across Africa and beyond while delving into the past for the major reason that it would be difficult to understand how the present came into being without seriously investigating the past. Also, it would be difficult to speculate trends in the near future without making reference to the past and the present. This is because the past informs the present while the present in turn informs the future.

To start with, All human societies in spite of their varied ideological backgrounds, have laws written or unwritten that guide and regulate the behaviour and contact of their members.Superficially, it appears law, policing, and morality refer to one and the same thing only said in different terms: they all deal with 'dos' and 'don'ts' backed by threats of sanctions of some sort. This understanding is normally buttressed by the fact that law and order are said to go together. So is policing and peace; morality and harmony.

Many people who do not and those who have never studied law, jurisprudence, criminology or legal philosophy, however, tend to have haze notions of the matrix and bonds that connect policing with law and morality.Singling out policing, the American sociologist, Egon Bittner (1974: 17) observed more than three decades ago that 'the police service

1

is one of the best known but least understood public institution'. In Zimbabwe, for example, crime and policing together with allegations of malpractices such as corruption, embezzlement, extortion and so on continue to feature with a thud in the press and television programmes, both the print and electronic media. Through all these varied forms of media, reports, and stories, policing in Zimbabwe as elsewhere in the world, has become known even by the village "lay people" in the so-called marginalised and underdeveloped areas.

Yet being familiar with policing should not be confused with understanding of what policing is all about, how it ought to be done, how it relates with law and morality, the role of and responsibility of the police service and so on. Many people, thus, remain with vague notions of what policing entails and especially the responsibility and role of police in society.

In view of this realisation, this book aims to do the following:

i). Conceptualise law, morality and policing;

ii). Explore the relationship of policing with law and morality;

iii). Offer different perspectives on what law, morality and policing is;

iv). Give an overview of what police service does and is expected to do.

These objectives are sought out on the pretext that some people are even contented with the little knowledge they have about the relationship of policing with law and morality. Yet, as the adage goes 'little knowledge is always dangerous'. The haze ideas that people have about law, the role and

2

responsibility of police, importance of policing and morality in Zimbabwenecessitate meticulous and rigorous analysis of the concepts of 'law', 'policing' and 'morality' in isolation.We in fact note in this book that while a close relationship and connection exist between law, policing, and morality such that each of the three depend on the other in one way or another, striking differences could be established as soon as we carefully unpack the concepts separately.

Policing: Nature and history

The concept of 'policing' could be fully understood after carefully unpacking the concept of 'criminal justice' of which it [policing] is part. As Brian Byers (2002) notes, criminal justice is admittedly a hybrid discipline drawing from many academic fields, some of which include social anthropology, cultural studies, psychology, and philosophy. It comprises such components as law, ethics, and policing. As a system, criminal justice comprises practices and institutions of governments directed at upholding social control, deterring and mitigating crime or sanctioning those that violate laws with criminal penalties and rehabilitation efforts (Walker 1992). Criminal justice system consists of three main components: legislative (create and reinforce laws), adjudication (courts), and corrections (jails, prisons, probation and parole). Our main concern in this section is the latter – policing, which is the first contact a defendant has with the criminal justice system.

As reported by Emsley (1996: 3), policing is from the Greek word *politeia* which meant all matters affecting the survival and wellbeing of the *polis* (city or state). Nowadays, the word policing refers to the policies, techniques and practice of a police force in keeping order, preventing crime, and maintenance of peace (Collins Concise Dictionary, 1988). Historically, the word and idea of policing were, however, developed by the Romans to justify the authority of the Roman Prince over his territories.

Alastair Dinsmor (2003) reports that the first police force to engage in policing comparable to the present-day police was established in 1667 under King Louis XIV in France, although modern police usually trace their origins to the 1800 establishment of the Marine Police in London, Glasgow Police, and the Napoleonic Police of Paris. As Emsley (1996) further elaborates, by the early 18th century in continental Europe, the words *la police* and *die Politzei* were being used in the sense of the internal administration, welfare, protection, and surveillance of a territory. The word *police* was not popular in Europe especially England as it was smacked of absolutism and linked with politics. However, towards the end of the 18th century, England and other English speaking countries of Europe increasingly used the word *police*. By police, we mean 'a constituted body of persons empowered by the state to enforce the law, protect property, and limit civil disorder' (Police Studies Institute, n.d.). The powers of police include the legitimised use of force, which makes policing normally but erroneously identified with force.

Underscoring Emsley's explanation of the link between policing and politics in classic Europe, Michael Rowe (2007: 4) asserts that:

> The word "policing" is etymologically related to "politics", the governance of the city or state and was used in broad terms to signify social regulation in the widest sense. The term "policing" did not come to be associated with the particular activities of a specific institution (the police force) until relatively recently in many societies.

4

Throughout history, different perspectives have been associated with the term "policing". A traditional (common sense) perception of what policing is reveals that it is primarily a matter of law enforcement. This perspective, as we note in this book, however, falls short in that it does not account for the many other aspects of police work and the dynamism associated with policing.

Another perspective of policing focuses on the routine functions performed by police officers. This perspective just like the common sense perspective of policing falls short in that it does not recognise the role of other institutions that are partners in policing. Also, it does not relate policing to the role of the police service in terms of the broader functions of the criminal justice system. We argue in this book that policing should and cannot be left to the police alone to decide. Our argument here stated resonates with the Commissioner of the Metropolitan Police (CMP) of Britain, Ian Blair's (2005) of policing who in his November 2005 public lecture suggested that 'increasing social diversity, debates about moral relativity, and social fragmentation meant that policing could no longer be left to the police to decide on their own'. We argue with Blair that the public should decide together with members of the police force what kind of police service is needed in their society. There is need for a generative dialogue between the public and the police.

Our position here stated does not only enjoy support from authorities such as Blair but from renowned scholars such as Michael Rowe. As Rowe (2007: 5) posits 'policing is not just the business of the formal police service as other institutions play a crucial role in developing, for example, public perceptions of criminal or deviant behaviour'. For this reason, Rowe alludes to the fact that it is difficult to pin down where policing begins and ends especially when viewed from this broad sense of the word and the sense that policing cannot be understood in isolation.

For the purposes of understanding what policing is especially in the context of Zimbabwe, we shall in this book, narrow the role of policing to the police service, in this case the Zimbabwe Republic Police (ZRP). Yet even with this pronunciation, we constantly make reference to the wider dynamics of policing and other such institutions that make policing feasible and an exercise worth supporting.The question that remains unanswered perhaps is: "why policing?"

Why policing? A brief look at Africa and Europe before colonialism

The world-over deviance is a normal phenomenon in human societies. Basing on the adage that 'no man is perfect', man always violates the laid down rules and regulations. At times, violation is perpetrated intentionally andvolitionally with punitive intentions while at times man finds himself trapped in situations that find him with no option but to get away with crime. Whatever the motive and gravity of the crime, violation of laid rules has never been celebrated since time immemorial. Even biblically, Moses found himself fleeing Egypt because he had killed. The propensity to commit crime is virtually in all individuals including the policemen themselves.

Early communities everywhere have also sought to maintain communal order and to correct as well as discipline those who depart from communally owned and acceptable behaviour, which explains why Chief Chirau of Mashonaland Central in Zimbabwe used to subject perpetrators of various crimes to ants (*mamhatsi*) as a way of correcting their uncelebrated behaviours (Personal Communication). This is because in many African societies, policing or crime management and control was chiefly a local community affair.

Parallels could also be drawn with societies elsewhere outside Africa. In the largely rural population of pre-industrial Europe, for instance, crime control and order maintenance was a local community affair. Policing was fulfilled by collective tasks and sometimes also through voluntary community service on a rotating basis (McMullan 1987; Draper 1978; Salgado 1977;Baker 2008:10).

According to McMullan (1998:95):

> The basic weapon that citizens of the early modern era learned to use to defend their security and combat danger was their intense sociability – a complex of human relations and institutions predicated on collective,local, informal and voluntaristic reactions to disorder and law breaking [...]. As a concept, police was a community duty.

The formal provision of policing through political authorities came later both in Europe and Africa. The shift from collective responsibility to a public policing system parallels the rise of state power in Europe and the desire to centralise and monopolise the forces of coercion under state control.Yet even as the European concept of state policing was being forged over centuries of state development, urbanisation, and industrialisation, private policing both communal and commercial never fully died out. This is in spite of the fact that histories of policing have generally overlooked the various ways policing was done in Europe.

The concept of state controlled policing came to Africa with colonisation following the Berlin Conference of 1884.In colonial Africa, policingwas however meant to safeguard the interests of the colonisers as they exploited the resources of Africa. The state controlled policing whether in Africa or Europe has, however, failed to achieve the state monopoly of policing due to their inadequacies.

While policing was a collective responsibility during the period before the 18th Century, this position was challenged by the social and economic changes that descended by the 18th Century. These challenges included urbanisation, industrialisation, and populations growing as predicted by Thomas Malthus. These challenges meant that many, for example, in Europe were left destitute, unemployed, and homeless, giving rise to numbers of vagabonds begging and stealing.It was no longer sufficient for a local community to undertake the responsibility for watching the conduct of each other.

As a result of this development, personal interests began replacing public spirit as the motivation of communal control.Without centralization of the policing machinery, it was not going to be easy dealing with the challenges.

The political classes of France were one of the first in Europe to appreciate the need for strong central control, through policing, to contain social unrest and migrant populations looking for work and the threat posed by them and others to the state. During the late 1700s and throughout the 1800s the country, France, saw revolutionary upheaval, coups, uprisings, wars industrial unrest, food shortages and rapid rural change (Popkin 1990; Hanson 2007; Doyle 2001).Inevitably the state was focused on how to maintain its order and to suppress rising political threats.

The army was not acceptable as a means of internal control, nor were the local civilian security provisions. There was need to come up with something acceptable to assume such an important role. Though provincial towns and cities had local forces (known as *Sergeant de ville*) and rural areas employed '*gardes champetres*'to enforce rural codes, these local security organisations were thought to be too localised and, inefficient and not sufficiently independent of local *revalues*(Furet 1995; Frey and Frey 2004; Hunt 1984; Paul 2007). They were unable to cope with social groups like vagrants, gypsies, escaped fellows and deserters or with more violent crimes like highway robberies, murders and riots.

The state found it a wise idea to have a centrally organised military force which had sworn its allegiance to the state and which unlike local security forces was armed, mobile, efficient, disciplined, and above local influence. It sought a coercive force that penetrated the whole nation and brought the state's demands, authority and norms to the people.It would be the one to deal with all the perpetrators of the defined crimes such as riots and tax evasion.

As the revolution and social unrest led to a review of French policing, city riots and rising crime in England led to similar calls for a state *sponsored* policing system, but one that was civilian, full time, public based and that could both keep the peace using minimal force as well as prevent and detect crime (Paul 2007; Hunt 1984).

While the state hesitated to take this step, private initiatives were undertaken. The Marine Police Establishment was a private police force set up in London in 1798. Its sixty armed men financed mainly by the West India Company, kept surveillance of the docks and warehouses along the River Thames. Two magistrates at Bow Street, London set up in 1750 a body of paid full time constables to detect and arrest criminals known as Bow Street Runners (Baker 2008). Though paid a salary, they were also hired out as private security guards and bounty hunters.With the British parliament's reluctance to provide a state authorised force for

London, the Bow Street runners expanded in number though never to more than 450 men in London of about 1.5 million people. They also began undertaking both foot patrols and in an effort to curb highwaymen, mounted patrols in the rural margins.

Whilst states in Europe, as part of their nation building project, sought to centralise authority for all aspects of policing within a single state body there was reluctance in England since it was a country where there was widespread suspicion of state control interference, and jealousy of civil liberty (Baker 2008). Centralised and militarised policing was suspect, thus when in 1785 William Pitt asked Parliament to create a police force in London it was rejected, being seen as too much like the French system.

The success of London's Bow Street Runners and other private policing initiatives enabled Robert Peel [the then Minister of the Interior] to successfully introduce the 'new police' in 1829.They, according to Baker (2008), began as a uniformed full-time force of 1000 officers responsible for a seven mile radius from the centre of London. They were unarmed, exemplifying their civilian character and policing by consent. Anxious that local authorities should accept greater responsibility for law and order, the British State introduced legislation that allowed, urged and then compelled boroughs to establish town police forces (Davey 1983).

Many scholars (Baker 2008; Davey 1983; Hunt 1984; Paul 2007) argue that it was the threat posed by the disenfranchised and economically marginalised 'dangerous' classes at the beginning of the Industrial Age that galvanised Europe's political classes into creating the police institution and giving it a mandate to secure public space through various legal instruments armed at public disorder, theft and violence of any kind. Civil police certainly filled the vacuum left by increasing restrictions on the use of capital punishment and of the military in internal affairs. The role of police force in the mid 1800s in England was, on behalf of local populations [or rather property owning ratepayers] to maintain the peace and watch [if not protect] private property. This role, however, meant that those outside the property owning classes were not so enthusiastic about them. Indeed the unpopularity of the British Police with the working class led to frequent violent attacks against them and protests to preserve:

Popular recreations or customs, prevent interference in strikes, protect wanted individuals, protest against police interference in political activities, protest against instances of police brutality, rescue arrested persons (Storch 1975:95).

It was not long before English ratepayers came to expect their local police forces to regulate their local communities more extensively, as poor law relieving officers, inspectors of nuisances market commissioners, impounders of stray animals, inspectors of weights and measures, recorders of animal diseases, controllers of vagrants and inspectors of common lodging houses, shops and licenses (Steadman 1984). Their activity was in other words done as much in accordance with local bye-laws as with natural statutory legislation, using if necessary, the legitimate use of force that had been granted to them.

By the mid-19th century inconsistent provision and a need for universal inspectorates led central government in London to oblige provincial communities to organise police forces and undertake crime prevention and local administrative roles. The processes had begun whereby local police forces came to be regarded as agencies of central government as well as or rural local magistrates and town watch committees.

11

Yet whether from the local or central perspective policing in the late 19th century was still concerned as much with population surveillance, control, local administrative services and civil law, as with the use of repression and force to curtail crime and uphold criminal law.such a diverse workload was not sustainable and by the 1880s the mood had changed and the call was for police who were professionals in investigating criminal offences.

From the foregoing, it is clear that policing has always existed to deal with perpetrators of the various pieces of legislation. Thus the police force has always had a role to play in society.

The role of the police

As underlined above, the police force has always had some role to play in society, particularly in the maintenance of peace and order. In Zimbabwe, Section 219 (1) of the New Constitution of Zimbabwe clearly states that: 'There is a Police Service which is responsible for- a) detecting, investigating and preventing crime; b) preserving the internal security of Zimbabwe; c) protecting and securing the lives and property of the people; d) maintaining law and order; and e) upholding this constitution.

Implication of the Section 219 (1) provision
The provisioned outlined above has the implication that:

- All civil disturbances of whatever form have to be dealt with by the police.
- All forms of crime must be prevented.
- If crime occurs it must be properly investigated. A properly investigated case leads to a conviction and

12

perpetrators will be given appropriate sentence. Sentence given depends on the gravity and severity of the offence and the amount of evidence available.

- Detection of crimes should be made possible through effective use of the various community policing initiatives in place such as the home officer scheme, NWC, suggestion boxes, hotlines.

In view of the Service Charter which is a comprehensive document that seeks to advise the public on the standards they ought to expect or demand from the police the role of the police is also defined as a marketing tool or strategy that links up the public and their police as equal partners in the war against crime. With regard to this initiative the role of the police also extends to:

➤ Assistance to the public, for instance, counselling services
➤ Conflict resolution
➤ Career guidance
➤ Crime awareness campaigns
➤ Certification of documents.

The above means that the police is there to serve the community. Lee (cited by Mayhall 1985:3) puts this clearly when he notes that 'police officers are public servants in the fullest sense of the term'.He goes on to argue that it should be understood at the outset that the principal object to be attained is the prevention of crime. To this great end, every effort of the police is to be directed. The absence of crime will be considered the best proof of the complete efficiency of police. What Lee says agrees with Cohn (1978:10) who argues that the primary purpose of a police department is the preservation of peace and protection of property against attacks by criminals. But how could this be possible?

Police-Public ideal interaction

Mayhall (1985:3) who cites Critchley (1967) and Reith (1952) tells us that 'when Sir Robert Peel undertook the reform of the London police with the Metropolitan Police Act of 1829, he and the two Commissioners that he appointed, Charles Rowan and Richard Mayne emphasised that the police should work in cooperation with the people and that members of the force should protect the rights, serve the needs and earn the trust of the population they policed'.

Sir Robert Peel had the conviction that the police-public interaction was the bedrock to eradicating crime. With such interaction no amount of challenge would be insurmountable. Together the police and public would create a sustainable working relationship. This entails that police officers should desist from the use of force when dealing with members of the public. As Feltoe (1998: 40) reminds us 'the United Nations Code of Conduct for Law Enforcement Officials provides in Article 3 that law enforcement officials may use force only when strictly necessary and to the extent required for the performance of their duties.' As Feltoe further explains, this provision means that the police must not resort to short cuts such as the use of more force than absolutely necessary in order to achieve legitimate law enforcement objectives; the use of force should be the exception rather than the rule and the police must only use a degree of force that is proportional to the harm threatened. In fact,

The duty of the police is to discover the truth. Their investigations into criminal activities must be fairly and objectively carried out. The police must obviously try to apprehend as many guilty persons as possible so that they can be duly punished. The public is rightly concerned about criminal activities, especially serious crimes. The police operate under substantial public pressure to apprehend criminal culprits. Investigating officers are also under pressure from their superiors to produce positive results, and police officers know that a good success rate will help when it comes to promotion. *Yet, a good rapport between the police and the public should always be maintained by both parties* (Feltoe 1998: 38; emphasis original).

With this understanding the police would be in a position to deal with the people in a professional and effective way. No police force is more important than the people it policies. To this end, we argue that police officers who prioritise police without people at heart can be compared to a 'poor' rich man who would rather bank his money for meagre returns than invest it in property for a bumper harvest, benefits that comes along with relationships and cooperation. This invites police officers to negotiate and reconcile the apparent tensions between what David Graeber terms an emphasis on 'maintaining a permanent sense of mutual obligation' on the one hand, and 'the denial of obligation and a maximum assertion of individual autonomy' on the other (Graeber 2001: 219), by providing for greater flexibility and cooperation in which 'closed relations can become more open, open relations more closed' (Graeber 2001: 220).Every police officer therefore should deal with members of the public as equal partners first and foremost in the life we received from the same Creator, where all men are equal.

Police officers in Zimbabwe as elsewhere are, thus, expected not to abuse their uniforms to satisfy personal gains or rather for personal aggrandizement. On the same note, the public is encouraged not to view the uniform negatively. Many officers on duty have been abused by the public; they have been belittled or have had their authority undermined (Personal Communication 2015). This is not good as it cultivates the hostility and widens the rift that normally obtained between police and members of the community especially during the colonial era in Africa. Such general hostility has in some instances caused bitter clashes between the parties. The public have ended up victims upon the police reacting to such negative perceptions that the people have about the police. This, if likened to physics, Newton would say, 'to every force there is always an equal and opposite reaction'.

Both the police and the public in Zimbabwe as elsewhere beyond, are fast forgetting the philosophy of Ubuntu that for centuries now has acted as a cushion for peace and harmony in Africa. The police now forget that they are police because of the people and the people likewise forget that there is peace and order in their societies because of the presence of the police. The public is made to live at peace with each other because of the police. This resonates well with Francis Nyamnjoh (2015) who using the Ivorian adage that: 'It takes one man to make another man' has this to cites the character Donmayer's reply to his helper, Chinto:

> I know it's because of you that I achieved success, but in life, it takes one man to make another. If someone is president, it is thanks to the people. If someone is a minister, it is thanks to the President. If someone is director, it is thanks to the Minister. If someone is secretary, it is thanks to the Director.

16

So, in conclusion, it takes one man to make another, thanks to someone we become somebody." Donmayer here will acknowledge the support from Chinto unequivocally, explaining that the latter is the one who "made" him, and in turn, he would "make other men" because, after all, "It takes one man to make another". He added that "in life, it takes one hand to wash another ... I know you're my saviour, but such is life." "If anyone has succeeded in the transport business (a type of businessman commonly called *Doulacthê* in Côte d'Ivoire)," continues the song, "owning several vehicles, it is thanks to passengers boarding his buses. If someone is the driver of these vehicles, it is thanks to *Doulacthê*. If someone is an apprentice driver, it is thanks to the driver. So in conclusion, "it takes one man to make another."

We, thus, underscore that while the police have so much power vested on them that includes the power to exercise discretion, this has also been abused by some officers in pursuit of selfish ends. Sometimes police officers rush to make an arrest well even before making the necessary investigations. They forget or perhaps are unaware that an arrest deprives the person his/her fundamental right to freedom and liberty. Feltoe (1998: 39) aptly captures this when he warns:

Any arrest deprives the person of his fundamental right to freedom and liberty. To arrest a person is therefore a drastic step and should not be resorted to unless it is justified. The power of arrest should be exercised sparingly, reasonably and responsibly. The Constitution of Zimbabwe provides in section 13 that no one may be wrongly deprived of his liberty. This right is subject to exceptions. One of these exceptions is that a person can be deprived of his liberty upon reasonable suspicion of his having committed a criminal offence. Where a person is unlawfully arrested he has action for damages against the arresting officer and the Ministry of Home Affairs.

The encounter and exchanges between the police and members of the public should, therefore, be equal if we are to have a 'real' peaceful and orderly society. This equal encounter entails that a police officer should always ask himself/herself before any arrest whether it is lawful or not.Ideally, the police, according to Lee (1985) are simply a disciplined body of men specifically engaged in protecting masses as well as classes from any infringement of their rights on the part of those who are not law abiding. The public on the other hand ought to be acquainted with the conditions that govern the mutual relationship.

The police force, particularly that of Zimbabwe, has in the recent years been forced on finding and securing common ground with the community. The more common the ground the more workable the relationship is. This can be represented by the following representation, figure 1:

Figure 1: Police-Public Intimacy

Police   Public

As is represented in the diagram above, the ideal relationship between police and the society would be a scenario where the police is more into the people and community is more into the police. With this position no task would be unchallenged, unmanaged and crime would be brought to a check. The police and the community would share the same vision and use their collectively owned resources to better all parties. Yet while this example of how police and the public must relate is very good and ideal, the situation that obtains on the ground is that the police is there to enforce the law which more often than not is breached by some of the members of society hence society cannot fully cooperate with the police. The other reason that may cause society to disengage with the police is the way they are treated by the police especially if one becomes the first to see a dead person. They are in most cases harassed, if not beaten, for having seen the dead body. One of our interviewee in Masving Province, Tatenda (not his real name) had this to say of the police:

Many a time people fear to report such cases. Something must be done to correct this dented relationship. As long as the relationship between the police and the public remains antagonistic like that of a cat and a rat, crime cases would continue escalating. In my view, there is need for a generative dialogue between the public and the police with a view to come up with a workable solution to the current predicament. I am happy that you noted and discussed this crucial aspect below. The two parties equally shoulder the blame. The police should not distance themselves from the community but should work as an extension of the community. In this way the community may be willing to work and cooperate with them in ensuring that peace and harmony prevail in society (4 May 2015).

As observed by Cohn (1978), there is no doubt that the police suffer from the fact that their role has been misunderstood. But the police frequently contribute to this level of misunderstanding by their lack of concern, unwillingness to share information and/or lack desire to involve the general citizenry in policy formulation and implementation. The police too, often view themselves as in conflict with the community, adopting 'we-they' attitudes rather than recognising the joint mandate the police and the community have in combating crime. This is normally a result of the fact that some members of the police force do not know some of the country's important pieces of legislation. This is very worrying considering the role of the police in society; that of enforcing law and order.

While it is imperative that the police and the community work together, it appears, however, that the community and police will never have a good working relationship. To this effect, Cohn (1978:14) asserts:

> No matter how efficient a police force may be and no matter how careful it is to observe civil liberties of long standing, it will always have to fight its way against an undercurrent of opposition and criticism from some of the very elements which it is paid to serve and protect. This is the enduring problem of a police force in a democracy.

According to Cohn, if there should be any progress in policing it is prudent to resist any efforts or programmes that will continue the isolation of the police from the mainstream of society. This is important given that the anatomy of society at present is so integrated that all entities on the life scene cannot afford to sideline each other. Co-existence has become so critical if the success, peace, and order that people cherish should be achieved, both as police or civilians. Gone are the days when the police was regarded lowly because of their level of education. Society used to look down upon it though they would fall back on it in the event of crime. Today so many police officers are commanding respect at various levels of society with the advent of college/university education and training programs tailor-made to capacitate the police with requisite skills and knowledge so as to remain relevant to the society policed.

The Police-Public Intimacy Theory thus holds that a sustainable and enduring spirit of working together of the citizens and police will better define the police mission, determine the best processes for programme implementation, find ways of educating, improving performance and productivity and thereby consolidating the chances of combating and controlling crime. Harmony between the public and police in terms of exception will ensure the positive development, growth and serenity for all parties.

The participation of these parties as proposed by this theory should be non-cosmetic, cosmetic just like fast bloomers is short season, fast bloomers do not last long, yet the relations required for an effective crime management stance requires and can thrive only on perennial relations. A non-cosmetic relationship can be buttressed by non-militaristic mentality on the part of the police officers. This is because being too hard on the public does not help anyone especially where people are conscious and would voice if there is a feeling that their rights have been violated or infringed.

One important point to make before moving on to the next section is that, in view of the theory enunciated above there is need, at least by the government, to make sure that both the police and public should be given a platform to review their current relationship with a view to come up with a positive and result-oriented working model that will assist in combating crime.

Law

As highlighted in the preceding discussion, many people conceive law as 'commands of some of powerful bullies who threaten to harm us unless we comply with their wishes' (Ingram 2006: 1). We consider this the first fallacy in 'layman jurisprudence': a misconception that needs correction. This correction is important as it allows people the opportunity to, at least, distinguish motivations of 'bulliness' from the quest to achieve order and peace in society. While bullying is more inclined towards 'unreasonable' and 'morally' unjustified commands, laws are reasonably motivated and justified at least in logical terms. Besides, laws can pass the logic of morality: they are morally justified at least in the society they are applied. We give example of laws that prohibit murder and adultery. Such laws, though commanding people not to behave in certain ways that rob particular members of society their rights to life and peaceful living, they express some logically reasonable and morally justified commands. This is not to reason that all laws are morally justified. There are cases where law commands people to do that which they think is morally wrong and logically unreasonable. The tradition that all children born twins should not be allowed to leave:a tradition that in the past was revered in many African societies, is a case in point. According to this tradition and the law that supported it, it was unlawful to allow children born as twins to live, yet looking at the tradition or law as it were it was morally unjustified. Neither was it logically obligatory at least in the eyes of a logical positivist. Such instances make the subject of law a fragile ground to be treated with caution.

To make the subject of law even more complicated, some laws are judgmental in so far as they express judgements nothing more nothing less. Such laws cannot be said to be actually commanding or authorise anything at that or this given moment because they are specifically about particular cases that might have happened in the past. The consequences or outcomes of the past cases (or actions) are here used to prohibit or permit a present action.

The subject of law is further complicated when these judgements appeal not to the official law-maker but to the authority of tradition and custom as in the case of the so-called 'traditional societies' for their legal standing. The same complication obtains when the judgements are applied to certain contexts, societies or countries where they may not even be recognised.

All these complications and others that are not here elaborated, point to the fact that law has no one universally defining feature, though of course, it 'designates something like an ideal that fully applies to only core instances of what it entails' (Ingram 2006: 2). These problematiques suggest that law can be viewed in varying degrees. In fact, what could be universally agreed is that law even used in different contexts has some overlapping resemblances: it has the essential feature that makes it recognisable as a law in the same way human beings have essential features that define them as humans different from other creatures.

That said, what then remains of law? Put differently, what then is law? Is it something abstruse, illusory or elusive as is the case with many other philosophical concepts?Before making an attempt to respond to these questions, we should point out that the task of defining law is one of the oldest problems in the philosophy of law with which most courses in jurisprudence or discipline related to law begin with. As such, the present book is not an exception given the focus and thrust of its contents.

One may, however, wonder why such a task of understanding law is necessary given that we all know that law exists and should be obeyed.What then is so special about law that it warrantsserious analysis and careful unpacking right at the outset of any reading or course that philosophises law? This question takes us back to the questions we raised above.

Now a response to some of these questions could be sought out from an explanation given by the nineteenth-century English philosopher of law, John Austin. Austin distinguished between what he called analytical jurisprudence and normative jurisprudence. For Austin, analytical jurisprudence concerns itself with the logical analysis of the basic concepts that are normally found in law as a subject such as the concept of law itself, duty, unusual punishment, equal protection, obligation, negligence, responsibility and others. Normative jurisprudence, on the other hand, deals with the rational evaluation and criticism of legal practices. The criticism in this case, though basically moral, could assume varying dimensions such as psychological, economic, political, social, religious or academic. It should be pointed out, however, that 'the philosopher who is interested in the moral evaluation of the law will be concerned with the nature of moral reasoning and argument and will be concerned to identify where such reasoning has an application within or to the law' (Murphy and Coleman 1984: 1). This is to say that the philosopher concerned with the religious analysis of law, for example, will not be obliged to give religious advice as such but will mainly be concerned to comprehend the logical structure of such advice and also to discover to what extent such analysis helps evaluate legal practices.The above explanation shows that whether analytical or normative, the primary task of law is analytical or conceptual. Jurisprudence and philosophy in particular is necessary to at least clarify concepts, articulate and maintain the logical standards of rational criticism including giving a rational account of usage of some concepts.To elucidate our point, we give the Longman Dictionary of Contemporary English (2009:985) definitionof 'law' as:'the system of rules that people in a particular country or area must obey'. Yet while such definitions given by dictionaries such as this above reports or tells us how people normally use certain words, dictionaries do not clarify the concepts with the rigour and dexterousness that philosophersof law do.

For scholars like Hart (1961), law has the following essential features that define it while making its analysis sufficiently difficult:

i). Law is clearly a devise for social contract: it is a device for getting people to do things that if left to personal inclination alone they would be unlikely do. It is this tenet that makes people sometimes confuse law with morality and even mere force. In fact, it is this overlap between law, morality and force that makes the concept of law more complex.

Yet while law could in a way identified with force, critical reflection shows that such identification is misleading even though there might be some elements of force present in many laws. What distinguishes law from force is that law is legal while force on its own is illegal. An example of a rapist's action of demanding sex from an unwilling woman is an act of force and clearly not legal in nature. This example makes it clear that though force might be closely related to law, it cannot be identified with law. What remains a fact, however, is that the relationship between law and force provides one reason why the concept of law warrants sufficient and careful analysis.

ii). The concept of law is ambiguous, one reason why law is in most cases confused with morality and sometimes with force. The ambiguity of law comes to light when people sometimes speak of laws in descriptive terms – descriptive law – that is statements of how things regularly happen in real life as is known from accumulated human experience. Newton's law of universal gravitation and Kepler's law of planetary motion which describes the motions of planets are good examples ofdescriptive laws.So is the law of conservation of energy which states that energy cannot be created or destroyed but only changed from one form into another or transferred from one object to another. For instance, when a kicker kicks a football that is sitting on the ground, energy is transferred from the kicker's body to the ballthereby setting it in motion. Descriptive laws are object of study of philosophy of science.

On other times, people speak of law in prescriptive terms – prescriptive laws – that is 'authoritative statements about what should or ought to happen or about what should or ought to be permitted to happen' (Murphy and Coleman 1984: 8). No one shall kill another under whatever circumstances is a hypothetical example (given that death penalty and termination of pregnancy are permitted under certain circumstances as contained in section 48) we can give of prescriptive law. It is a statement of what the state or people are permitted to do or not to do.Prescriptive laws are

26

an object of study of discipline such as jurisprudence or philosophy of law.

iii). The concept of law require an analysis in terms of elements such as rules which are equally philosophical. In fact the question of what a rule is and what it means is as philosophical as the concept of law itself. It is for this reason, among others, that Hart (1961) concluded that though the concept of law is indispensable in society, it is interestingly difficult to unpack such that it requires philosophical examination and rigour.

Yet, South African lawyers, Hahlo and Kahn (1968) try their best to simplify what summarises law to us when they say it [law] is a rule recognised and enforceable by the state. Hahlo and Kahn, thus, assert:

[T]he next question we have to answer is: what distinguishes the law of the lawyer [...] from other practical laws, such as moral law, the laws of etiquette or the laws of cricket? The answer is that law in the strict sense is the only body of rules governing human conduct that is recognised as binding by the state and, if necessary, enforced. This does not mean that there are no sanctions as far as other practical laws are concerned. There is the conscience of the individual, the pressure of public opinion, social approval or disapproval. But only law in the strict sense is enforced by the courts of law or some other organ of the state (p. 3-4).

Morality

The concept of morality is frustratingly vague: it has been a bone of contention among moral philosophers for a long time now. As a matter of consequence, the concept has been notoriously understood, explained and interpreted differently

27

even among moral philosophers themselves; hence rendering it an essentially contested concept and everybody's game.

Plato in his Republic relates the question of morality to justice. He understands morality in much the same way he understands justice which he defines as 'that which is done to the advantage of everyone and not to the advantage of the stronger' (Findlay 1993: 31). We should, however, comment that Plato's understanding of justice (as morality) is only achievable in theory and not in practice as it has been argued and convincingly so by Thomas Hobbes that human beings by their very nature are egoistic.

In Kammer's conceptualisation of morality and a just society, we find a similar understanding as that of Plato. Kammer (1988: 7) had this to say: 'the fact that we are moral beings defines our humanness'. Kammer, thus, understands human beings as moral agents based on their intellectual capacity to subject their and other people's actions to critical examination and logical scrutiny.

For other scholars such as DeGeorge (1982: 12), 'morality is a term used to cover those practices and activities that are considered importantly right and wrong, the rules which govern those activities and values that are imbedded, fostered or pursued by those activities'.As Mawere (2011: 10) and critically unpack the above understanding of morality, 'it implies that ethics is the philosophical study of morality: ethics' object of study is morality'.

Now that morality is at the centre of ethics, it is peremptory that we understand what is meant by ethics.

According to Popkin and Stroll (1972: 239), 'ethics is a set of principles or a set of rules which sanction or forbid certain kinds of conduct'. For example, when speaking of policing one has to bear in mind some set of principles which regulate the conduct of policing. This means that ethics has a bearing on one's character.

Basing on Popkin and Stroll's understanding of ethics, William Shaw (1999: 4) defines ethics as 'that which concerns individual character, that is, how we ought to behave'. Ethics, thus, speculates about good life, a peaceful society, or a world worth living. It is all about the ought – the dos and don'ts or what is good, bad, right or wrong in life.

Yet while many people agree on what ethics is, they tend to disagree when it comes to what constitute that which is considered as good, bad, right or wrong. This difficulty makes ethics (as morality itself) a complex concept which like the concept of 'law' requires careful analysis and usage. However, given that the goal of ethics and morality is not only one and the same but the object of ethics is to study morality, we, in this book, use the terms 'ethics' and 'morality' interchangeably.

The logical relationship of law, morality and policing

While a relationship between law and morality has been explored by some philosophers of law (see for example Ingram 2006; Madhuku 2010; Hahlo and Kahn 1968; Murphy and Coleman 1984), to date, little has been done to interrogate how law and morality relate to policing. The need for interrogation of such a relationship is, therefore, more urgent than ever.

The relationship of policing with law and morality cannot be underestimated. The relationship is not only practical but logical: it is a logical necessity needed, even imperative, to foster peace and harmony while propagating a world worth living by all.

As dictated by natural law theories originally developed by such ancient philosophers as Plato, Aristotle, Cicero and St Thomas Aquinas, there is an essential connection between law and morality. Lovemore Madhuku (2010: 3) captures this aptly when he asserts:

Law is law, regardless of its moral content. However, most legal rules arederived from morality. This means that in such instances, the law is usedto enforce morality. Lawmakers seeking to enact new laws to regulatehuman conduct usually convert into law their deeply held moral convictions.Morality is the bedrock of law but it is not law.

To illustrate his point, Madhuku gives an example of the Biblical-cum-moral rule: 'Thou shall not kill' which he argues is a rule of morality such that if the state decides to recognise it, it also becomes a legal rule, but if the state decides not to convert it into law, it remains a moral rule only.

We add that the referred essential connection of law and morality do not only end with the relationship betweenthe two [law and morality]. It extends to the realm of policing. We claim that there is an essential connection existent between law, morality and policing. The demands of law, morality and policing more often than not overlap such that policing as law itself has to pass a moral test for it to be considered as 'good' policing. This is not to reason that policing, morality and law are equals as there are many policing and moral obligations that have no place as legal requirements. Courtesy gratitude by individuals is a case in point.

Likewise, many legal and policing requirements do not, in their content, represent moral obligations. A legal requirement that 'Summons' be signed by an individual being sued do not, in content, represent moral obligations. This is not to dismiss the fact that the relationship or connection between law, morality, and policing is a logical necessity. The truth remains that no law count as law unless what it requires or demands people to do is in itself morally permissible in the context the law is being applied. The same logic applies to policing. No policing count as policing unless what it requires people to do is at least morally permissible in the context policing is being exercised. No wonder St Augustine had it in his natural law slogan that 'an unjust law is no law at all' (see Pegis 1948). We add it that unjust policing is no policing at all. Putting it in other words, moral validity is a logically necessary condition for both policing and legal validity. This is to say: One is obligated to police against murder, for example, in as much the same way one is obligated to obey the law against murder simply because murder is wrong in itself (*malum in se*). Murder is in itself morally wrong: murder is not wrong because it is prohibited (*malum prohibitum*). Also, moral validity is a logical condition for a peaceful, harmonious and worth living world such that immoral law and unprincipled policing are respectively no law and policing at all. A philosophical analysis based on simple logic shows that:

Premise 1: Both law and morality deal with principles by which men in any society live.

Premise 2: Law and morality are central in policing for a peaceful and orderly world.

Conclusion: Therefore, policing cannot do with law and morality.

It is out of this syllogism that our analysis of law and morality as they relate to policing is feasible and indeed hinged.

In view of this reasoning and as already underlined in the preceding discussion, we argue that policing unguided by law and morality is like a misguided missile directed towards humanity to cause more harm than it should prevent. This reasoning finds homage in James Madison's argument that 'only a society of perfect angels would not need a government; they would need no morality for they would not have to place restraints on their behaviour as we (humans) do' (see Grassian 1992: 12). It also finds support in Hobbes' claim that men by nature have egoistic tendencies that disrupt the society on which their life and happiness depend through, among other things, competition for resources, pride, grudge, and jealousy.

Hobbes' claim has the implication that if left unchecked, unlike in a society of *perfect* angels (and not ordinary angels like the one third that followed Satan on his revolt against God) envisaged by Madison where harmony and peace flourish, the aforementioned tendencies would result in what Hobbes called a state of war, 'such a war as of every man against man. In such conditions, there is no place for industry because the fruit therefore is uncertain and consequently no culture of the earth' (Edwards 1960: 430). This affirms that law, morality and policing are a necessity for peace, order and harmony. Besides, the trio coexist for the survival and good of both society and the policing service itself. This understanding can be represented by the diagram below, figure 2:

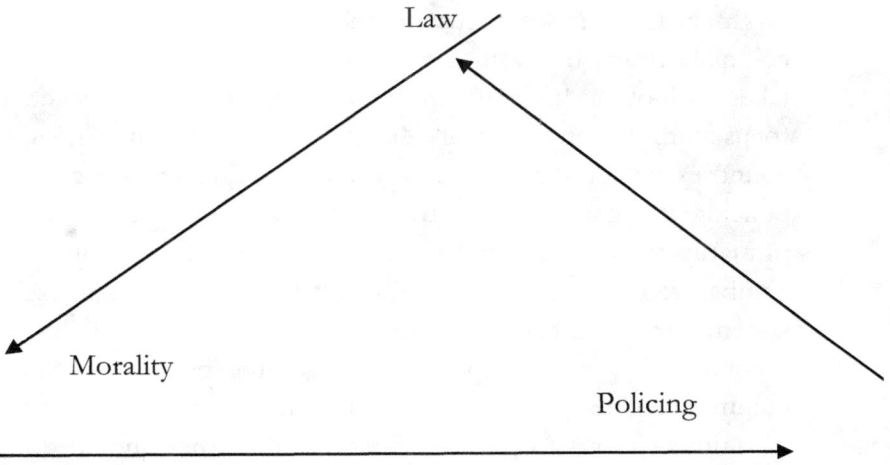

It should be underlined that the relationship of policing with law and morality is that of interdependence. Each of the three depends on each other.

While the dependence between law, policing and morality is indispensable as has been demonstrated so far in the preceding discussion, we underline that the present text is more inclined towards policing: it is more of a handbook for policing. This is not to undermine the relevance of the present text to other such disciplines as philosophy of law (jurisprudence), criminology, and moral philosophy. What one should bear in mind is that the main objective of this book is to promote policing informed by morality while at the same time equipped by law. It is our reasoning that law without policing is like a clanging cymbal, yet law without morality is empty. It is only when the relationships between law, policing and morality are satisfied, that we can talk of good policing in society, and in our case, in Zimbabwe.

As this chapter is an introduction to the book, a brief summary of their contentsmight be helpful.

In chapter 2, we focus on the criminal justice in pre-colonial Africa, but with a focus on Zimbabwe. Chapter 3 takes a look at policing in colonial Africa. It, however, focuses more on colonial Zimbabwe and South Africa, countries which are studied as examples. Chapter 4 tackles policing in post-colonial Africa. Yet, given that this book primarily focuses on Zimbabwe the chapter's focal point is Zimbabwe.In chapter 5, we focus on the criminal justice system in Zimbabwe, particularly the responsibility, accountability, and compliance of both the police and the communities being policed. The last chapter is more of some recommendations to police officers on how they should do their policing in a changing environment as that of Zimbabwe.

Chapter Two

Pre-colonial Criminal Justice in Africa, with a focus on Zimbabwe

Introduction

While Euro-centric scholarship of pre-colonial Africa is awash with the propaganda that pre-colonial Africa was uncivilised, there is ample evidence across the continent that many institutions as those existed in the so-called civilised Europe also existed in pre-colonial Africa. The institution of criminal justice, one responsible for policing is one such institution that pre-dates colonialism in Africa.

Using scholarly literature on the history of criminal justice in Africa, this chapter traces the history of criminal justice before it challenges and unseats the Euro-centric and pro-colonialist propaganda that led to the assumption that it is European colonialists who brought criminal justice, law and order to Africa through its civilising mission and initiatives. In this endeavour, the present chapter makes the argument that criminal justice as a system with its quest to obey law and promote peace and order in Africa predates colonialism on the continent, yet little in terms of research, has been done in the area of criminology to look at the historiography of criminal justice, especially policing in pre-colonial African societies such as Zimbabwe.

Africa and the question of Criminal Justice

In the past four decades, the discipline of criminology has grown immensely especially in the English speaking countries of Africa, Western Europe and America. This situation still obtains in many parts of Africa but with a dominance of western-biased criminology. The dominance of Western criminology in Africa means that more examples in criminology studied on the continent are drawn from the West than anywhere else in the world. The dominance also perpetuates the Euro-centric propaganda or myth that it is Europe that brought a sense of criminal justice to Africa. There is, therefore, dearth of literature on criminal justice and policing in particular that focuses on Africa especially during the pre-colonial period. The scarcity of literature on criminal justice in Africa is however relative with some societies in Africa, for example, West Africa now beginning to advance seriously in the area of criminology (see for example, Onuwudiwe 2000; Dalgeish 2005; Ebbe (ed) 2000).Dalgeish (2005), for example, studies criminal justice in Songhai Empire of West Africa. He found out that in this part of West Africa existed criminal justice well before the advent of colonialism in the area. Yet this should not be mistaken to be reasoning that Africa is homogenous. The modern countries that were covered by the then Songhai Empire include: Gambia, Guinea-Bissau, Senegal, Mali and large parts of Niger, Guinea and Mauritania and small parts of Sierra-Leone, Cote D'Ivoire, Benin, Burkina-Faso and the northern part of modern Nigeria known as Hausaland (see Dalgleish 2005: 59). As further pointed out by Dalgleish, the Songhai Empire was the largest West African civilisation ever witnessed and was famed for its many educational institutions. Walker and Millar (2000: 49) detail that 'the subjects taught at higher education level in Songhai Empire included mathematics, accounts, logic, grammar, Islamic law, astronomy, geography, poetry and art'. This is a clear testimony that education in Songhai Empire was no less equivalent to that offered in modern-day universities even though Walker and Millar did not highlight the distinct high achievement in Songhai Empire and therefore its contribution to world civilisation. Dalgleish (2005) further claims that Songhai Empire had an organised government and administrative system consisting of a member of ministries such as agriculture, etiquette and protocol, cavalry and minority, among others (Diop 1987: 124). In Songhai Empire, cases thus were tried and those convicted punished.As Lady Lugard (199: 199-200) wrote of some of the punishment that was common in Songhai Empire: 'There was a state prison for political offenders, which seems to have served a purpose similar to that of the Tower of London and the courtyard of the prison of Kanato was no less famous in local annals than Tower Hill'. Diop (1987: 126) also reports of some annual punishments in Songhai Empire which though rare were actually instituted. These included being buried alive inside a sewn-up bull's hide. This 'unusual' punishment could be equated to that of Britain's during the same period. Farringdon (1996: 26) reveals more on this when he says:

> The penalty (in Britain) for not attending church in the time of Henry viii was the loss of one or both ears. His son and successor, Edward VI made the crime of brawling in a church or churchyard punishable by mutilation. Poor standards of hygiene meant that the punishment of mutilation was tantamount to a death penalty for many.

Hunwick (1999) just like Diop (1987) used documentary evidence of a number of Arab scholars such as Kati (1913) and Sadi (1993), African scholars whose work dates back to the 16th century, to advance the argument that criminal justice existed in Africa prior to the advent of colonialism.

Even prior to the existence of Songhai Empire, Levtzion and Spaulding (2003) document that as early as the 11th century, when travelling in Ancient Ghana, Al-Bakri referred to the king's 'Court of Justice'. Levtzion and Spaulding (2003) further report that Al-Idrisi, writing a century later after Al-Bakari, also in Ancient Ghana, spoke of the 'widely known justice' of the ruler, Takruri. Al-Idrisi even went on to write of another king in Ancient Ghana:

> One of his practices in keeping close to the people and upholding justice among them is that he has a corps of army commanders who come on horseback to his palace every morning. When all the commanders have assembled, the king mounts his horse and rides at their head through the lanes of the town and around it. Anyone who has suffered injustice or misfortune confronts him, and stay there until the wrong is remedied. His riding, twice every day, is a well-known practice and this is what is famous about his justice (see Levtzion and Spaulding 2003: 32-33).

According to Levtzion and Spaulding (2003), in the 14th century, Al-Qolqashandi mentioned judges, magistrates, and jurists with reference to the king of Borno in north-east Nigeria. Also, in Mali in the 14th century, Ibn Khaldun wrote that 'Mansa Musa, a king in Medieval Mali, was an upright man and a great king, and tales of his justice are still told' (Levtzion and Spaulding 2003: 94).

All this, is evidence to demonstrate that administration and governance in many parts of Africa had similarities with Western systems especially Britain. In some cases, some African societies even went beyond governments of their

European counterparts of the same time. A case in point is Songhai Empire. Songhai went beyond its European counterparts in that it provided ministries for minorities – catering for small ethnic groups – in its kingdom. Such ministries were non-existent in Europe during the time.

Centralised kingdoms in pre-colonial Africa, however, did not only exist in West Africa. In ancient Egypt, for example, existed centralised governments. In the Nubia and Axum Empires in North East Africa also existed centralised kingdoms, while Zimbabwe Empire existed in Southern Africa. All these were large kingdoms or empires that developed complex systems of governments. They were in many regards similar to kingdoms and empires in Asia and Europe that were in existence during the same time. As already alluded to, other empires in Africa even went beyond their European counterparts.

In other African societies such as Zimbabwe, although the discipline of criminal justice is studied in many tertiary institutions and the development of policing exists, the area of criminal justice remains under-researched: there is still much dependence on the Western-biased criminology thereby perpetuating the pro-colonialist and Euro-centric propaganda that criminology in Africa is a foreign phenomenon. This calls for the need especially of those in the mainstream criminology in sub-Saharan Africa and Zimbabwe in particular to invest more in the history and comparative study of the subject besides other such dynamics associated with the discipline. This makes the present work a milestone towards introducing and furthering investigation in the history and theorisation of criminal issues in Africa.This is not to say no effort at all is being exerted by scholars in the country. Lovemore Madhuku (2000), for example, in his book: *An introduction to Zimbabwean law*, tackles some important questions around issues to do with the legal system in Zimbabwe. Augustine Runesu Chizikani (2010) also looked at the legal system, particularly commercial law, and the title of his book is: *Commercial law in Zimbabwe*. Chizikani, thus, discusses the different principles of law, cases, statutes, and authorities applicable in Zimbabwe.

We should however, underline that even those Zimbabweans who have examined issues around criminal justice and policing in Zimbabwe in particular have largely used the lens of Eurocentric theories that do not only reject that criminal justice existed in pre-colonial Africa but that law and policing and the order that comes along with the latter are not a gift offered in a silver plate by colonialism. We argue, in this book, that the continual viewing of criminal justice with the spectacles of Euro-centric theories do not only perpetuate pro-colonial theories but dehumanises and drags back the people of Africa into the yoke of slavery and mental colonialism. Such viewing also furthers earlier Eurocentric scholars' views such as those of Hegel (1956) who in one of his celebrated works had this to say of Africa:

> The peculiarly African character is difficult to comprehend, for the very reason that in reference to it, we must give up the principle which naturally accompanies all our ideas – the category of universality. The Negro exhibits the natural man in his completely wild and untamed state (p. 93).

What worries even more is that while the need for accurate historiography on pre-colonial Africa is more urgent than ever, the imbalances that occurred during colonialism are likely to remain, as they have always been, because further work is normally inhibited due to lack of funding.

This chapter ultimately aimed at finding evidence from the works of authors who researched and wrote on pre-colonial criminal justice in Africa in general and Zimbabwe in particular. However, the fact that much of that literature is Eurocentric in nature, having been written by scholars who either worked or were linked to the colonial administration of the time, we borrow our evidence from oral literature and literature from disciplines other than history of criminology such as ethnology, social anthropology, history, and archaeology, among others. This literature helps us in many great ways to debunk pro-colonial and Eurocentric stances on criminal justice, and to understand policing and sociological crime control in pre-colonial Africa.

While the sections above examined criminal justice in pre-colonial Africa in general, this section focuses exclusively on pre-colonial policing and crime control in pre-colonial Zimbabwe. This emphasis is done on the pretext that the present book deals with criminal justice and in particular policing in Zimbabwe. Yet, we underline that for us to understand criminal justice system and in particular policing in pre-colonial Zimbabwe, we need to explore, though briefly the history of Zimbabwe before colonialism – the history of Zimbabwe Empire.

History of Zimbabwe before colonialism

Zimbabwean history can be traced to as far back as the first Bantu speakers to arrive in present day Zimbabwe, who were the makers of early Iron Age pottery belonging to the Silver Leaves or Matola Tradition of the third to fifth centuries AD found in south-east Zimbabwe (Huffman 2007: 23). From archaeological findings at Gokomere, it is believed that the Bantu in present Zimbabwe migrated from the north

41

eastern part of Africa and modern day south-eastern Kenya and north eastern Tanzania and then southwards to Mozambique before they moved on to south eastern Zimbabwe and Malawi, then to Natal, south Africa and finally to the Zimbabwean plateau. This was around 1000 AD. More substantial in numbers in Zimbabwe were the makers of the Ziwa and Gokomere ceramic wave of the 4th AD (see Huffman 2007).

A later phase of the Gokomere culture was the Zhizo in southeastern Zimbabwe. Zhizo communities settled in the Shashe – Limpopo area in the 10th century. Their capital was called Schroda just across the Limpopo River from the modern day Zimbabwean side. The inhabitants produced ivory bracelets and other ivory goods. Imported beads found at Zhizo sites are evidence of trade probably of ivory and animal skins with traders on the Indian Ocean.

Bantu languages at sites in north-east Zimbabwe of around 7th century suggests that the makers of Ziwa/Gokomere wares were not the ancestral speakers of the Shona languages of today's Zimbabwe, who did not arrive in there until around 10th century. They were migrating from south of the Limpopo River and with ceramic culture belonging to the western stream (see Hufman 2007). The linguist and historian, Ehret believes that in view of the similarity of the Ziwa/Gokomere pottery to the Nkope of the ancestral Nyasa language speakers, the Ziwa/Gokomere people spoke a language closely related to the Nyasa group. Their language was, however, superseded by the ancestral Shona languages, although Ehret says that a set of Nyasa words occur in central Shona dialects today (see Ehret 2001: 239). The evidence that the ancestral Shona speakers come from South Africa is that the ceramic styles associated with Shona speakers in Zimbabwe from the 13th century to the

42

17th century can be traced back to western stream (Kalundu) pottery styles in South Africa (see Huffman 2007).

Although the western stream Kalundu tradition was ancestral to Shona ceramic wares, the closest relationships to the Shona ancestral language according to many linguists (Holden 2002; Gythrie 1967; Fexova etal. 2006; Ehret 2001) were with a southern division of eastern Bantu such as Nguni, Sotho-Tswana, Tsonga, Nyasa and Makuwa. After Shona speaking people moved into the Zimbabwean plateau, many different dialects such as Kalanga developed over time in different parts of the country. It is believed that the Kalanga speaking societies first emerged in the middle Limpopo Valley in the 9th century before moving on to the Zimbabwean Highlands. The Zimbabwean Plateau eventually became the centre of subsequent Kalanga states. The kingdom of Mapungubwe was the first in a series of sophisticated trade that later occurred with European explorers especially from Portugal.

From about 1250 until 1450, Mapungubwe was eclipsed by the kingdom of Zimbabwe. The Kalanga state further refined and expanded upon Mapungubwe's stone architecture, which survives to this day at the ruins of the kingdom's capital of Great Zimbabwe. From circa 1450 – 1760, Zimbabwe gave way to the kingdom of Mutapa which stretched to modern day central Mozambique.

The Mutapa Empire later on collapsed in the early 17th due to a series of war instigated by the Portuguese settlers (Martin and Silliman 2005). As a direct response to Portuguese aggression in the interior, a new Kalanga state emerged called the Rozvi (the destroyers) Empire who drove the Portuguese from the Zimbabwean plateau by force of arms. The Rozvi continued the stone building traditions of the Zimbabwe and Mapungubwe kingdoms while adding guns to its arsenal and developing a professional army to protect its trade routes and conquests.

The RozviEmpire was later on weakened by the Zulu's Mzilikazi of the Khumalo who rebelled against Shaka around 1821 and created his own kingdom, the Ndebele. The Ndebele and later European settlers led by Cecil John Rhodes weakened the Rozvi empire and led to the destruction of the Great Zimbabwean kingdom. The Great Zimbabwe kingdom had a criminal justice responsible for policing, administering of peace and order. In the next section, we focus on the pre-colonial community policing and criminal control in Zimbabwe.

Pre-colonial community policing and crime control in Zimbabwe: Debunking the myths, setting the records straight

Community policing is a concept that has failed to come with a single and precise definition. While this is the case it is now so common in various communities across the globe because of the numerous exploits that it comes with. Yet community policing could be better comprehended after the word community itself. The word policing has already been looked at in chapter one.

Community

Community is derived from the Latin word *Communis,* which means fellowship and the concept of 'community' has been derived as being the fundamental and far reaching pillar of society as it fosters a feeling of warmth, intimacy and sharing of common values (Nesbitt 1970). A community, thus, is a group of people who leave in sympathetic proximity with to a greater or lesser degree, some significant factor in common (Alderson 1982).

Community Policing

Community policing is a philosophy and an organizational strategy that promotes a new partnership between the people and their police (Trojanowicz and Bucqueroux, 1994). As further articulated by Trojanowicz and Bucqueroux (1994), community policing is based on the premise that the police and the community must work together as equal partners to identify, prioritise and solve contemporary problems such as crime, drugs, fear of crime, social and physical disorder and overall neighbourhood decay, with the goal of improving the overall quality of life in the area.

For Peak and Glensor (1997: 78) community policing is the dominant direction for thinking about policing designed to reunite the police with the community. Peak and Glensor, thus, agree with Trojanowicz and Bucqueroux that community policing should emphasise good relationships between the police and the community.

Basing on the understanding of community policing above, However, community policing has also been viewed as a 'plastic concept' which means that a plethora of communities, individuals or scholars view it differently. Yet, basing on the understanding of community policing elaborated above, it is clear that while community policing appeals to different people in different fashions the main pillars of the concept thrust on the fact that community policing emphasises that:

➢ a well-knit and positive relationship is the starting point between the police and the community.

➢ the people and police ought to share the same vision in view of the problems in the community.

➢ the officers on the ground must be willing to work and committed to ensuring a crime free community.

➢ resources must be availed to ensure that achievement of the goals is a realistic undertaking.

➢ being reactive is more costly than being proactive.

But isn't that community policing is a modern phenomenon which came on the scene in Africa after the wave of colonialism?

As noted by Osaro Ollorwi (2013), and rightly so, crime is not a modern phenomenon nor was it restricted to areas of 'civilisation' and greater differentiation in pre-colonial Africa. Crime has always been a common phenomenon in pre-colonial African societies.

In pre-colonial Zimbabwe, as elsewhere, people always committed crimes of different magnitudes. This prompted the need for community policing to ensure peace, unity, and harmony.Mawere *et al* (2013), in one of their ethnographic novel about the VaDuma people of south-eastern Zimbabwe, revealed that each crime committed in the Duma society had its own sentence depending on its gravity and circumstances around it. As Mawere *et al* (2013) narrate: in the Duma Chiefdom each criminal act had its own sentence depending on the gravity. While thieves had their palms cut or *short sleeved*, witches and wizards, for example, had one of their ears cut and in most cases suffered exorcism. Adulterous men had their sexual organs cut such that they would never again engage in adulterous acts.

Chapter Three

Policing in Colonial Africa south of the Sahara: The South African and Zimbabwean Experiences

Policing in a colonial state

When the European settlers came to Africa they were in pursuit of their so obvious agenda which according to Gibbs, Phillips and Russell (1981) was a chance of de Beers or its off shoot to acquire a country with exclusive rights to profitable investments. In such a country, the colonisers knew that with the wealth they would acquire, they generate power and vice-versa. To ensure that their cause stands out they had to establish and advance a colonial rule to help them maintain order in view of their background, interest, and needs.

This realisation gave birth to the police and military forces which in all respects had to ensure that the new'masters' were protected and their needs and interests always advanced. To these forces the prevention and detection of crime was secondary as their primary role and mandate was to take care of the business of the colonial master of the time.

Baker (2008) rightfully notes that as the territorial boundaries of the colonial regime were secured and peace largely prevailed, the emphasis of colonial rule inevitably began to shift from military – political security to civilian control using the state police force. With their urban focus, the police handled violations of the newly introduced European Criminal Codes in areas of European settlement. Not surprisingly, many of the new laws were meant to secure political stability (through subjugation of masses) and served the economic interests of the colonial power. Much of the police work was involved in the surveillance of European property and persons. In view of this Bouman (1987) reports that the Bechuanaland Police were accused of only being interested in offences under the Masters and Servants Act and the Liquor Act, and in later years offences under the Native Pass Law and the Native tax Act. In other words, what Bouman is telling us is that the force was hardly interested in criminal behaviour unless whites were involved or affected.

Basing on these findings and reports, it could be well argued that the role of the police then was regime policing, policing the colonial economy and upholding the authority of colonial rule (Young 1988). This meant, of course, that the white coercion was not used continuously but it would be reserved for use when deemed necessary. We therefore argue that this coercion was meant to instil psychological conditioning in those where the force was used. As Young (1888: 47) tells us, not only did the Europeans use armed policing, but just as importantly, they equipped themselves with a 'legal arsenal of arbitrary regulations to carry out (their) responsibilities, that is the Master – Slave ordinances, specified periods of obligatory labour service at state defined tasks, plenary powers to local administrators to impose penalties for disobedience.'

Policing and nationalism

The suppressive hand of the European settlers through the manipulation of the police was also instrumental in thwarting the rise in nationalism in many African countries such as Zimbabwe. The police was brutal, insensitive and could not compromise the colonialists' principles. This continued to hurt the black people between the 1930 and 50s. As a result of this treatment many positive and conscious blacks started engaging in politics in a bid to free themselves from the colonial bondage.

The police remained the ultimate tool to suppress such moves and for those who were apprehended the police was the tool to effectively deal with them.The political order the conscious blacks were advocating for brought even more suffering till a protracted war of liberation was ensued to liberate Zimbabwe. The idea for the blacks was to usher in a new order, a new philosophy that would cascade through all the institutions so that Zimbabwe would be one big family with the police being a people's force.

This new order would bring policing by popular participation. This position would ensure unity of purpose between the police and its various publics through its ranks and files. But how such kind of policing could be possible in a country where foreigners had invaded the land, now in full control of both the resources and the people?

Views/Paradigms on Policing

Neo Feudalism

When private policing was rediscovered in the mid 1970s in North America and a little later in the United Kingdom private and public policing were sharply divided with the former being primarily thought of as commercial security.

After an initial interest in security guards, research on private policing began to note gated residential communities, mass retail outlets, and sporting or leisure complexes that suggested fortified fragments where a privately defined order was administered by private security.

It was an order where undesirables were excluded through methods other than state law and largely through the consensus of participants and the design of the environment.In other words, some exclusive communities/spaces were arising where a different order of law and its administration was applied to that of the state in public places.The parallel was drawn with feudal society and that of mediaeval city states, since the fortified enclaves of privilege deployed a system of exclusionary justice.However neo feudal paradigmsuggested a clear-cut separation between private and public orders of policing that did not fully fit the world of overlapping and co-operative patterns of security.

Multilateral Policing

According to Bayley and Shearing (2001), multilateral policing is characterised by two distinct layers, namely auspices and provider of policing. This is because, for Bayley and Shearing, the roles of state and non-state policing often overlap. In fact, while auspices are groups that explicitly and self-consciously take upon themselves the responsibility for organising their protection, providers are the groups that actually do the policing asked for. This results in the coinciding and sometimes clashing between auspices and providers. A defining characteristic of the new paradigm of policing, however, is that auspices and providers may not be the same (Bayley and Shearing 2001) even though they sometimes coincide.

Bayley and Shearing's (2001) review suggest that policing is authorised by a variety of sponsors; economic interests (formal and informal, legal and illegal), residential communities, cultural communities, individuals and governments. Bayley and Shearing also believe that policing includes commercial companies, non-state authorisers of policing, individuals and governments. On the one hand, a variety of non-governmental groups and agencies have undertaken to provide security services.

As such, the boundaries between auspices and providers have blurred such both public and private entities have assumed responsibility for authorizing policing; both public and private entities provide policing to these auspices (Bayley and Shearing 2001).With the intervention and participation of non-state actors in many government activities, it is now well known that even government's role is no longer exclusively public. Many democratic governments now authorise policing, encourage non-governmental groups to authorise policing, and provide policing to specialised consumers on a fee for service basis. Similarly, private providers are no longer exclusively private given that in most cases they work under public auspices and are sometimes staffed by public police personnel.

The [re-]entry of citizens into policing functions, whether with or without the State police's blessing has also been noted by Johnston (1996; 2000). Commenting on the active role of citizens in both authorizing and/or providing policing, he writes:

> Citizens, rather than being the passive consumers of police services, engage in a variety of productive security activities. Such co-production ranges from individual/household activities undertaken with police co operation [properly marking, becoming a special constable] to those lacking such co operation [buying a fierce guard dog, surrounding one's property in razor wire]; and from group activities supported by the police [liaison groups, neighbourhood watch groups] to those denied such support [hiring a private security patrol to

protect a group of residences, engaging in citizen patrol] (Johnston, 2000:965).

Though it may be true that the boundary between public and private has lost its distinctiveness over time, some insist that collapsing the whole field of law enforcement is to merge phenomena that are inherently separate. There are indeed significant differences in the authority, organisational structure, legality and working definitions of communal deviance and order.Nevertheless both public and private policing have important features in common. They are both rules of coercion engaged to preserve internal communal order and they draw on similar control and investigative techniques.

Rural Networked Policing

This paradigm recognizes that the state is not [and cannot be] the sole source of both provisions and accountability in policing but emphasises the relationship and co-operation between the diverse policing groups. In other words, it is not that the boundaries between state and non-state institutions have blurred but that they have been transformed by new partnerships.

According to Loader (2000) who proposed the abovementioned view, policing groups are not to be seen as isolated autonomous groups but as together providing a security network across society.He talks of the network of power in which the state is but one node:To this end Loader (2000:323) argues:

This network continues to encompass the direct provision and supervision of policing by institutions of nation and local government.But it now also extends to private policing forms secured through government; to transitional police arrangement taking place above government; to markets in policing and security services unfolding beyond government; and to policing activities engaged in by citizens below government we inhibit a world of plural, networked policing.

This is a framework that recognizes a multiplicity of State, market and community groups loosely networked to provide shared control, order and authority.In this tradition some prefer to talk about security networks rather than policing.In a similar vein, Kempa *et al.* (2004) talk of a concept of policing as a process of networked nodal governance understood as a complex of interlaced systems of agencies which work together to produce order.The many permutations of private policing involve the forging of connections between numerous agencies to form extended networks of regulatory power.

Though many nodes are acknowledged, this paradigm assumes the primacy of state law and still regards the government as the primary node.This security network tends to be defined in terms of the variable relationships with the state.

More governments in recent years have been seen to encourage citizen participation in self-policing schemes and urging prudentialism (O'Malley 1997). These individuals are in effect being incorporated as private agents in a networked policing process, though with their central relationship still being to the state police.

Security Governance

This view was propounded by Johnston and Shearing (2003).It incorporates all the insights of the earlier paradigms, but is prepared to deny conceptual priority to the state in any security network.They argue that it is important to carefully separate what policing is in essence from the historical forms which policing has taken, in terms of its underlying mentalities and their related institutions, technologies and practices.

It has never between in dispute that traditionally policing has been about the application of punishment by state officers.However, this is not the only way of approaching policing.The current understanding is that policing also includes such facts as problem solving, risk management, remedial/restorative approaches operated through alternative institutions of the state, business or voluntary bodies.In buttressing their argument Johnston and Shearing defined security governance as, "the application of any means that will promote and secure places in which people live and work".

The universality of private policing

This is the only view that recognises Africa and was advanced by Christopher Clapham (1999).He contends that most African States have never developed public security systems in the first place, in the sense of security systems that protect all citizens without discrimination and which are accountable to them.Essentially, the state security systems in his view have been developed to support the ruling elite in their hold on power and wealth. Clapham sees no justification of retaining the dichotomy between public and private security. All security systems are private to the extent that they all serve the whole population. What however divides these essentially is the degree to which they are efficient and accountable.

Failing to find true public policing in Africa, Clapham abandoned the distinction between public [or State managed] security systems and private [commercial or even criminal] ones.His collapsing of all law enforcement into one category challenges those who claim public authority for state policing to prove that such forces serve the interests of all the citizens and are accountable to the public.To him it is not just that African policing groups, whether called private or public, may engage in similar activities [a point that could be contested] but that they have a similar purpose to promote private interest. We are left therefore with a spectrum of private security systems.Each system displays a combination of the two basic criteria of any security system: 'its efficiency in maintaining some kind of order on the one hand, and its accountability to those people whose security is at stake on the other'.

As can be noted, all these paradigms relate, though not in totality, in different ways to the policing system that was used in the colonial era in many African societies.

Policing in colonial Zimbabwe: Experiences from within

During the years Africa was writhing under colonial rule the continent remained underdeveloped in many respects. As articulated by Walter Rodney (1972), underdevelopment expresses a particular relationship of capitalistic exploitation whereby one society exploits another with the intention to enrich itself. There is no way a country can exploit another without instruments that make the exploitation possible. The underdevelopment with which the world is preoccupied is a product of capitalism, imperialism and colonialism. These systems were always anchored on policing and law, draconian or otherwise. Without an effective police and even army, there is no doubt that people would rise up against these repressive systems with bane and acrimony.

The indigenous people, from here onwards referred to as people, needed force to be whipped into line with the orders and commands of the masters so that the master continued to exploit resources in Africa without any fear.While some of the resources exploitedon the African land were used to develop the immediate environment, the larger part of the resources was shipped to Europe depriving the host societies of their wealth. This was made possible through policing by fear and intimidation. The laws were so brutal and draconian such that anyone who dared oppose the white men risked the consequences of being exterminated from the earth.Chaza (1998: 42, emphasis original) aptly captures this when he notes:

> I must not lose sight of the crude, good-for-nothing white policemen I regret to have had the misfortune to meet. For example, there was one trooper nicknamed John Blunder-buss, *who using oppressive laws of the colonial time*, his presence meant terror to both the native constables and the black civilians.

The masters were characterised by exploitation, brutality and psychiatric disorder as this ensured Africa remained backward while its resources developed Europe (see Rodney 1972).

During this era the whites were the minority across the face of Africa yet they controlled virtually all the resources, peoples, sectors, and institutions. In this vein Walter Rodney (1972:164) reports that 'colonial governments discriminated against the employment of Africans in senior categories and whenever it happened that a white and a black filled the same post, the white man was sure to be paid considerably more'. This was true at all levels from civil service including the police, army to mine workers. Rodney further argues that

African salaried workers in the British colonies of Gold Cost (now Ghana) and Nigeria were better off than their brothers in many other parts of the continent, but they were restricted to the junior staff level.

As already highlighted, for the European settlers to exploit the resources across Africa they needed security to safeguard their interests and make sure they would not face resistance from the people. The resources looted across Africa included gold, tantalite, diamonds (from Democratic Republic of Congo) Agricultural prime land, gold (from Zimbabwe), copper (mainly from copper-belt, Zambia), among others. Chaza (1998: 5) confirms this when he reports that 'the indigenous people saw their possessions, especially cattle, confiscated and their freedom curtailed'. Because of the heavy handedness by the security, the looting was done at a very large scale. This resulted in most of the African countries, though with the greatest amounts of natural resources, becomingthe poorest in terms of goods and services provided by and for their citizens.

The grip the settlers had on the locals was too tight. No wonder Chaza (ibid) had it that:

> Instead of cultivating good public relations with the indigenous people among whom they were going to live with, the settlers showed streaks of the most ruthless primitiveness when dealing with the indigenous people. They quickly strained their relationship with the people of the country.

The control ensured that any deviance by the blacks was immediately dealt with. To perpetuate their policing philosophy as indeed in other sectors, the white settlers occupied all senior and influential positions. No native policeman occupied a rank above that of Native

Sergeant(NS), which was a non-commissioned officer (also see Chaza, 1998).

The training within the police was two-tire which was a system biased towards perpetuating white supremacy and hegemony. In Southern Rhodesia (now Zimbabwe) training for black policemen was done at African Police Training School Depot (APTS), Tomilson depot (now the Morris depot or Morris Depot Police Museum).It should be noted that European recruits were not trained at the same place with the native recruits. The curriculum between the native and European trainees was different too because the latter were trained with the view of seconding them to leadership positions while the former were trained to be patrol men. They were segregated as was the case in other sectors of the economy.

The policing philosophy of the white commanders was fashioned to police the people by intimidation, fear, threats of violence, and force. The British South African Police (BSAP) in Southern Rhodesia as elsewhere in the face of Africa was a brutal force with terrorising menace of high magnitude.BSAP was the police force of the British South Africa Company (BSAC) of Cecil John Rhodes which became the national police force of Southern Rhodesia and its successor after 1965. Until 1899, the force also policed parts of BSAC territories north of the Zambezi River and now Zambia (see also Gibbs *et al* 1981). The police could beat, detain and even shoot without restraint. This reality is confirmed by a number of scholars (Gibbs *et al* 1981; Chukuma 2001; Chaza 1998) who researched and wrote on policing in colonial Africa. Chaza (1998), for instance, reports that 'the Blackwatch (native contingent) was commanded by one Captain Brabant, a ruthless man who shot dead many natives as punishment for refusing to bow to the whitemen's rule'. The policing thrust in Rhodesia was solely to ensure law and order prevailed using any tools at their disposal.During the Rhodesian Bush War in the late 1960s and 70s, for example, the BSAP formed an important part of the government's fight against nationalist guerrillas when it [BSAP] established a riot unit (or tracker combat team), later renamed the Police Anti-Terrorist Unit (PATU), a police field force type Support Unit who were distinguished by wearing black boots. The police only saw the public when there was trouble, a phenomenon known as crisis intervention (Muzenda who cites Schlicht 1998:18).

It was this brutality among other concerns that compelled nationalists to challenge the status quo.Wars were waged to deal with this system which was inhumane. Ultimately political independence was achieved in the whole of Africa. But how did this kind of policing found its way into the African societies? To answer this question, we need to understand the different paradigms on policing, particularly from the West where policing in colonial Africa was adopted.

Policing in Black Townships before independence: A case of South Africa

Before independence was granted to African states by their colonial masters or through protracted battles, clashes in black townships were very common. These clashes made policing very difficult since political resistance was the order of the day especially in many African communities. In South Africa, for example, this was even worse according to the Legal Education Action Project (LEAP) and Criminal Justice Resource Centre (CJRC) because the South African Authorities responded by instituting even hasher methods of repressing the blacks. Their argument was that 'to every force there is always an equal and opposite reaction' (Newton's law of Motion).

The clashes were more pronounced in the so-called Black Townships. During the period 1986-89, black townships were inhabitable. The crimes of all sorts were committed in broad day light: peace and tranquillity was nowhere in sight to be witnessed around townships. It appeared as though everyone had resigned to believing that chaos was now the new order and policing was now impossible.

In responding to the crime in black townships, the BSAP in South Africa introduced a special programme that was meant to promote peace and sanity in the townships. These black constableswere known as *Kitskonstables*which means 'instant constable.' This meant that they were inadequately prepared to assume that important policing role (Legal Education Action Project, and Criminal Justice Resource Centre). This crop of policemen was trained for six weeks only and dispatched to these high resistance areas. Thousands of these black constables were sent into these black townships where they policed by terror and were soon known for their reign of terror, brutality and lawlessness. They were also perpetrators of crimes themselves because they felt invincible and ultimate forgetting that noone is above the law.

What the deployment of these *Kitskonstabels* meant was that black policemen were actually deployed against their black brothers and sisters. They were also exploited, underpaid and isolated from communities, consistent with the views by Rodney(1972:164) who argues that exploitation by the settlers'was exploitation without responsibility and without redress. In 1934 for example, forty one Africans were killed in a gold mine disaster in the Gold Coast, and the capitalist company offered only £3 to the dependents of each of these men as compensation.' This is clear testimony that indigenous Africans were maltreated by their colonial master.

The police in colonial South Africa as that in colonial Zimbabwe was a two-tire force, the white policemen and the black policemen. For instance, the *Kitskonstabels*, as native policemen were called in South Africa, patrolled on foot in areas where the regular police (white policemen) only patrolled in armoured vehicles. The uprising that started in September, 1984 in South Africa made many black townships no-go areas for the police. The police, whether black or white, was thus an enemy of the people.

The state's repressive laws fuelled further hostility between the police and the people. As the people responded to the exploitative and draconian laws the police heavily descended on them with all their mighty and viciousness. Unfortunately on the part of the colonial government, the people could not be suppressed because of the consciousness they now had from the speeches of people like Steve Bantu Biko, Chris Hani, Robert Mangaliso Sobukwe, and many other Pan-Africanists in South Africa and beyond. People became more and more prepared to die in defence of their peace and freedom. Some of the policemen also died in the process (as is shown in the film – Sarafina).

The abusive behaviour and heavy handedness of the police created very bad blood with the public to the extent that the people responded with hand grenades as what happened in Nyanga and Kattlehong in 1987 (Institute of Criminology: University of Cape Town). Individual *Kitskonstabels* are said to have been stoned, stabbed to death and even shot at places such as Bongolethu, Lingelihle, Imbali, Botshabelo, Khayelitsha, Soweto and Gugulethu.

In response to the uprisings by the black populace the police introduced the state of emergency in which the police were given much wider powers to detain and use force. They were also given the power to shoot and torture suspects without fear of prosecution (Legal Education Action Project and Criminal Justice Resource Centre). Such brutality by the force negatively affected the image of the South Africa Police (SAP). In spite of the immense power the policemen had at their disposal, they dismally failed to contain the uprising which confirms that policing cannot be done effectively through the use of force.

The Police Force as a tool to advance colonial interests

It should be reiterated that when the colonisers came to Africa in pursuit of their so obvious agenda which, according to Peter Gibbs,Hugh Phillips and Nick Russell (1981), was a chance of de Beers or its off-shoot to acquire a country with exclusive rights to profitable investments, they did everything within their power to make sure that their goal was achieved. The country being referred to here isSouth Africa where it was believed that wealth would generate power and power in turn generates more wealth. To advance these interests while maintaining what they called 'order', the colonisers had to establish and extend colonial rule that was not only ruthless but selective when it comes to the use of the law.

The police and military forces had to ensure that their masters as well as the latter's interest were protected and safeguarded. To these forces the prevention and detection of crime came second. Their primary role was to take care of the security and business of the colonial master.Much of the police work was involved in the surveillance of European property and persons with little or no care was made on the security of indigenous Africans. Bouman (1987) captures this aptly when he reports that the Bechuanaland Police were accused of only being interested in offences under the Masters and Servants Act and the liquor Act, and in later years offences under the Native Pass Law and the Native tax Act: otherwise the force was hardly interested in criminal behaviour unless whites were involved.

Adding his voice to this reality McCraken (1986:131) cited a report by a Commissioner of Nyasaland, now called Malawi, who said:

> They are perhaps engaged in collection of hut tax, escort of cash, accompanying the District Commissioner on *ulendo* and other duties that might well be performed by a messenger staff. The actual position is that it is only the areas in the Southern Province where there is European Settlements that are policed.

This, perhaps as sure as day, confirms that the role of the police then was regime policing, policing the colonial economy and upholding the authority of colonial economy and the authority of colonial rule. Not only did the Europeans use armed policing, but just as importantly, they equipped themselves with a 'legal arsenal of arbitrary regulations to carry out (their) responsibilities, that is, the Master – Slave ordinances, specified periods of obligatory labour service at state defined tasks, plenary powers to local administrators to impose penalties for disobedience' (Young 1994:47).

Charges of vagrancy, prostitution, beer brewing, smuggling, poaching, loitering, native witchcraft were among those offences used to criminalise Africans to control their labour and to repatriate them to native areas. This, according to Baker (2008) enabled the police to tackle legalistically what it had previously accomplished militaristically. State law provided the technical procedures and the bureaucratic framework that enabled the police to rationalise their activities as law enforcement.

McCraken (1986) concluded that social and economic control did not make the police popular with the local population. In one of his publications: *'Culture and consumption: A theoretical account of the structure and movement of the cultural meaning of consumer goods,'* McCraken commented that one group of complainants to the Nyasaland authorities wrote that the average policemen not only carries out the instructions he is given but enters every neighbouring house and put everything in disorder. The African policemen were actually viewed as sell-outs and traitors of the Native African community. This negative view of policemen is not only unique to South Africa but can be seen from the way policemen were stoned in Accra, Gold Coast (now Ghana) as early as 1886.

As the colonisers pursued their goal of perpetuating white supremacy and dominance, there are times they evoked the State of Emergency as an instrument for repression or trying to reclaim public order. This can be seen in Nyasaland and many parts of apartheid South Africa where dissent was suppressed through shootings, detention without trial, collective fine, burning of houses and seizure of possessions (Killingray1997:181).

To preserve European domination police forces had to engage in military and political activities of surveillance, penetration and oppression of suspect groups (Killingray1986). Colonial policing in South Africa as elsewhere in Africa, thus, never followed the idealised European model of a civilian force living in the community. Under the colonial regime, policing in local communities was engaged in upholding the draconian laws irrespective of the

64

fact that the government that passed the law was in the first place illegitimate.

In fact, the police was basically the front line of defence to maintain law and order while the soldiers were the last and this has endured to present day. Today the police and soldiers work together in low intensity operations to contain public disorder. The colonial state was characterised by repressive, suppressive and oppressive laws that were indeed one-sided and selective. This means that the common saying that no one is above the law was far from reality in colonial Africa. There was ever present threat of violence, pain and suffering as law was selectively applied against indigenous people. Crowder cited by Baker (2008: 65) summarises the colonial state as one that:

> Was conceived in violence rather than in negotiation [...] It was maintained by the free use of it [...] It must be remembered too that the colonial rules set the example dealing with [...] opponents by jailing or exiling them, as not a few of those who eventually inherited power knew from personal experience.

Special powers and declarations of emergency could always legitimise setting aside the law if it was thought necessary or *defacto* immunity from prosecution could always be established. To this Chukwuma (2001:128) confirms this when he reveals:

The colonial government organised the police as instruments of riot opposition and suppression. They were not established as agents for promoting the rule of law, human rights, community safety or for delivering social services.

This is seconded by Chaza (1998: emphasis original) who on writing of policing in colonial Zimbabwe reports that:

The black policemen, *Mabhurakuwacha*, in colonial Zimbabwe, were employed to do all the dirty work of their colonial masters. Atrocious acts of tyranny were openly committed and the intention was to put fear into the minds of the 'Kaffirs'. The burning of villages, wanton murders and rape were so rampant that the perpetrators even regarded it as sport.

Revisiting Policing in Rhodesia (now Zimbabwe)

Rhodesia was a colonial state whose birth was seen with the hoisting of the Union Jack, a British flag, on the 13th September, 1890 at the Kopje in Salisbury, now Harare and the capital city of Zimbabwe. From this day on the state was divided into two major classes; the European settlers who took themselves to be masters and the natives whom the settlers took to be servants and at their [settlers] mercy as masters.

This scenario cascaded into many other institutions, the police included, which were meant to ensure security of the 'new masters'.In Zimbabwe,the native police force was formed in 1895 in Bulawayo, now Zimbabwe's second largest city,even though the native did not assume any meaningful positions in the force. And, a British South African Police force in which the blacks were included was formed in 1896 as a mounted infantry – Mashonaland Field Force (see Chaza 1998). The native constable was actually enlisted as a tool that could be taken to a scene of crime, and to perpetuate oppressive authority and tyranny of the colonial regime. The native constable was, in this respect, a mere tool just like the clipboard, pen, pencil at the disposal of the European attending officer, so to speak. He was defined as a Blackwatch (*Bhurakwacha*). The term *Bhurakuwacha* was 'a corruption of the English word *Blackwatch*, which was one of the pioneer occupation regiments of Queen Victoria of England' (Chaza 1998: 5).

The *Bhurakuwacha* was not only considered as inferior in the eyes of the settlers but in the early years of policing in colonial Zimbabwe, the black policemen were issued with uniform that was not user-friendly.It was a uniform that was used through all seasons. To this Chaza (1998:5) says:

> The Blackwatch regiments uniform included a very prominent garment – a black woollen jersey which had leather patches on the shoulders and elbows especially designed for the rough and tumble life it was meant to endure. This was the garment [...] worn by black policemen nearly everyday throughout the year regardless of the changes of the weather. It also served a pyjama-coat.

Yet the native police was formed with the sole objective to give comfort and security to the white settlers.Chaza (1998)even described black policeman as a symbol of oppressive authority and of tyranny to the indigenous peoplealthough he [black policeman] was viewed as an inferior being with no feelings at all.

Through the use of the police force by the colonial regime, the defenceless natives saw their possessions, especially cattle which,in fact, was a symbol of wealth and source of drought power confiscated and their freedom curtailed. The black police were actually defined as 'dogs of the white settlers' (*zinja zemakiwa*) by the Ndebeles (Chaza 1998: 5).

The white police officers never took effort to correct the relationship between the police and the public. They were not worried and did not care about the security of the communities they purported to be protecting. Not only were they unsympathetic to the public but also to the black policemen themselves. Chaza (1998:6) reveals '[...] the Blackwatch (native contingent) was commanded by one captain Brabant, a ruthless man who shot dead many natives as punishment for refusing to bow to the white man's rule'. He goes on to narrate his own ordeal as a BSAP member when he was forced by his white colleague to carry him on his back across a flooding river. Chaza (1998: 42), thus, narrates the ordeal which needs us quoting directly:

> I had a classical clash with one trooper nicknamed John Blunder-buss. We were riding a motor cycle when we got to a point where the dirty ox wagon road crossed the Mazowe River about two miles east of the main Bindura/Mt Darwin Bridge over the Mazowe River. Blunder-buss as wearing leather leggings and boots and I had none. He asked me to push the motorcycle through to the other side of the river. The motorcycle was too big and heavy a machine for one person to push through a rough passage with invisible boulders under water. However, I battled it out and crossed after what I think was a very taxing effort. Blunder-buss then asked me to come back to him on the other side of the river so that I would carry him on my back across the river. I took off my jumper, which was all wet with sweat, my cap and haversack and left them by the motorcycle on the other side of the river. I folded my pair of khaki shorts up to my thighs because the water was above my knees. When I got to trooper John Blunder-buss, he told me to get back to the other side of the river to put on the jumper because he could not hold my bare, black body. I did so unwillingly although feigning cheerfulness and within no time trooper Blunder-buss was on my back like a big child. I think he weighed about 90kg.

This is, however, not to say all the white policemen were this cruel. There were exceptions too, to quote Chaza (1998: 42):

I will appear very ungrateful if I do not eulogize Trooper Ginger Bourne whom I think is an embodiment of those few white policemen of the day who performed their duties in the manner good policemen should. It is to this category of policemen, to which Trooper Ginger Bourne belonged, that I must pay my warmest tribute for all the good they did to uphold the force's good name. However, I must also not lose sight of the crude, good-for-nothing white policemen I regret to have had the misfortune to meet.

The superiority of race dominated in the police force to the extent that a black policeman could lead a horse on foot while the white policeman rode on that horse. While the whitemen could wear shoes and leggings the black policemen walked barefooted (Chaza 1998). It was actually an offence for a black policeman to wear shoes. Even after recommendations from GMO, no native police policeman could wear boots. It was not acceptable at all to quote Chaza (1998: 88) who reports on his experiences as a native policeman that:

The warrant officer quizzed me about who had given me permission to wear boots. I told him that I had been given permission to wear boots from Police Headquarters PHQ on recommendation from the Government Medical Officer (GMO) from the district [...] the inspector overruled both the permission from HQ and the recommendations from GMO. He said he would not have a native policeman under his command wearing boots.

Great distances were covered on cycles by native police. These distances were covered during patrols or even on transfer. To this end Chaza (1998: 45) says 'I soon found myself on my indomitable Hercules bicycle heading for Goromonzi with all my worldly goods on the carrier. I was on permanent transfer'.

The story was different for the whitemen. These had all the comfort that was possible then and to this Chaza says '[...] in some instances the black policeman would carry the white boss on his back(see the narration above by Chaza himself). This was not only dehumanising, but annoying yet no black policeman could dare challenge that position.Even the accommodation of the black policemen was too bad by any standard especially as compared to that provided with the white policemen counterparts. To this end Chaza (1998:49) reports:

> The native police quarters at Goromonzi were of the same pattern as found in all police stations in Southern Rhodesia. You only had to see one for you to see them all! The N/Cpl (native corporal) allotted me one of [...]. Mine was the worst of them all. I found that there were bloody stains all over the wall, a clear sign that whoever had occupied it last had been at war with bed bugs and other blood suckers.

The white community also had no respect or empathy for the black policeman. They looked upon the black policemen as mere tools at the disposal of the white masters. To this Chaza (1998) writes:

> As I limped behind the *mujoni* (white man), dozens of automobiles zoomed past me with the drivers who were all whites never bothering to give a ride to the poor limping *bhurakwacha*! How I envied some poor half naked natives riding

on the back of a half tone truck looking after some crated pigs while a dog was occupying the front seat with the boss.

The native policemen were expected to commit themselves to their work even though the working conditions were unfriendly, inhumane, and in fact a thorn in the flesh. The conditions were so frustrating and disheartening, yet the conditions for resignation were not any better and Chaza (1998:62) adds:

> Because of these frustrations, I put in an application for immediate discharge from the infernal BSAP with its harsh dos' and don'ts and horse escorts! But I was reminded to fulfil first my contract of three years' service, or buy myself out by paying cash for the remaining period [...] I took a mental calculation of how much I could have to pay and found that I would not afford. So poverty forced me to battle on.

This goes to reveal and confirm that at times the native policemen remained in service out of poverty and will to serve in the force. Some of them were not enjoying the work at all. They had to endure all the same. The native policeman during this era was also charged with the responsibility of trekking down deserters from European farms. At times they were put on risk as they crossed flooded or crocodile infested rivers. This had nothing to do with crime, but advanced the interests of settlers yet the 'desertions were caused by poor conditions of work including beatings, inadequate food rations, and other deprivations at which the white colonial farmers were experts- exploiting the poor and vulnerable black' (Chaza 1998:72).

The concept of policing by consent was used in dealing with the white community only. Any report by a white man was handled by a policeman of no rank inferior to that of a Sergeant no matter how trivial.

What is worrying, however, is the fact that some of this inhuman behaviour is still inherent in some of the current crop of police officers and unfortunately the brutality is now directed to their fellow Zimbabweans. As suggested by one police officer, Constable Tagara (not his real name) in an interview in Masvingo (March 2015), this perpetuation of brutal tendencies of some police officers is possibly exacerbated by the fact that most of the Police Officers who survived the colonial brutality were upon attaining independence incorporated within the Police and most of them were promoted to positions of authority. As a result, some of them failed to adjust and correct the past injustices and in the process they unconsciously transferred the 'psychological genes of brutality' to the current police. This is evident in part of their training which by and large is still colonial in nature in so far as most of the drills given during the colonial era continue being used in training camps.

Chapter Four

Policing in Post-Colonial Africa: A focus on Zimbabwe

The work of Pan Africanists and nationalists such as Kwame Nkrumah, Julius Nyerere, Kenneth Kaunda, Joshua Nkomo, and Robert Mugabe, among others, ushered in a new dispensation in African governments. These nationalists and pan Africanists challenged the whitemen including many of their colonial systems, in many ways too numerous to mention. Yet challenging the whitemen has never been an easy thing: it has neverbeen an easy road to tread on. On realising that the road to freedom was littered with thorns, Nelson Mandela had to write a book *'No easy walk to freedom'* to chronicle the evils of the white domination in South Africa and other parts of the African continent.

The fight of the black man across Africa on various fora especially in the late 1970s forced the whitemen to negotiate peace agreements with the locals in some countries but in other countries protracted battles were to be fought. A good example of the latter is Zimbabwe which became independent in 1980 after a bitter war that claimed thousands of innocent lives. Political independence in Zimbabwe as elsewhere on the continent, was expected to usher in a new Zimbabwe with a new face in terms of governance, institutions, and administration.

Crime trends in some African states

Many African States are having a torrid time dealing with ever-increasing crime rates. The absence of equity in sharing the resources has caused a lot of evil minds to take toll among citizens. In some instances it is actually survival of the fittest that dictates the life of a society. Giving an example of what was happening in Togo in the recent past, Baker (2008b:31) who cites the Ghanaian Chronicle (28 July 2003) notes that 'most Togolese now literally go to sleep with at least one eye virtually open'.There is no one to protect them, no one to guarantee their safety and that of their property. The situation has been aggravated by the fact that the police has failed to rise to the occasion.The police force has been defined as unfair, disrespectful, inefficient and ineffective.To this end Baker says:

> The BBC's Africa Live programmer ran a series in September 2003 called Africa's police:'Friend or enemy?' where he invited listeners to evaluate their state police. The overwhelming number of respondents on their website responded negatively.

It was revealed in this BBC programme that many people across countries have no confidence in the police, since the police force has failed to justify their existence especially in time of need. People are at times mugged in their full view, traffic offences are flouted right in front of them as is the situation that obtains in South Africa. In the city of Johannesburg, for example, one can be robbed in front and full view of a police officer who would actually do nothing to help the victim (Personal experience 2011).Those officers who work under the traffic departments in South Africa and many other African countries are even more notorious and daring than the 'criminals' themselves, hence the question 'who will police the police?'As one of the Zimbabwean, Jairos who happened to have been in South Africa during the recent xenophobic attacks narrated:'people were burned and killed in full view of Police Officers, those who are paid to enforce law and maintain order in society. Instead of thwarting the menacing crowds the police were busy taking photographs. What a shame?' (Interview in Masvingo 7 April 2015).In fact, these officers are more criminals than the criminals that the officers pretend to be policing. To this end, the traffic police in Kenya are called TKK – *Toa Kitu Kidogo* – Swahili phrase for give something small (Backer 2008b).In Cameroon police are referred to as 'mange milles thousand eaters – in reference to the customary bribe of 1000 CFA'. In Zimbabwe, the police especially the traffic ones referred to as *vanaMayaya* – money harvesters – in reference to their habit of collecting bribes from motorists.

In Zambia, Assistant Commissioner of Police and Copper Belt Deputy Police Chief, Grace Chipahla, said there were many criminal elements within the ranks than perhaps there are outside (The Times of Zambia, Ndola 24 July 2003). The late President Mwanawasa of Zambia also expressed disappointment at the police service in his country that he said had failed and needed serious cleansing.

The inadequacies of the African police is disheartening yet could be the result of many factors among which are poor working conditions, low salaries, under-funding that itself has a political motive (Hills 2000), corruption amongst those who are associated with the state and possess the means of coercion (Bayart *et al* 1999), the result of lingering cultures of authoritarianism and disciplinarianism (Baker 2002a; 2002b), and the colonial origins of the police and decades of military rule that together produced militarised police forces that acted as instruments of oppression on behalf of the government.

Such observations and experiences have led scholars such as Shearing and Kempa (2000) to argue that the proven inability of the police to single-handedly produce security within the nation has created a vacuum in security. It is this vacuum that has caused crime to rise to unprecedented levels like fire in the Harmattan Winds. The African societies, which traditionally are communitarian and modelled on the principle of Ubuntu, have been seriously fractured and the social fibre that used to tie them together no longer prevails. The society is now a jungle where all 'animals' ought to be vigilant lest they will not see the next season.

Africa is currently viewed as the most violent continent in the world on the basis of crime (UN-HABITAT Safer Cities Programme 1996). According to one survey carried out in Uganda, South Africa, and Tanzania, three Africans out of four in the cities had been victims of violence during 1999-95 (UN-HABITAT Safer Cities Programme 1996). This is nearly twice as many as in the cities of Asia and South America.

In many African countries, crime rate seems to be increasing day-by-day. Malawi's official crime statistics show that reported crime increased steadily between the years, 1995 – 99. Between 1997 and 1999, for example, the number of reported armed robberies rose by nearly 40% while the number of murders per year increased slightly (Baker 2008b:36).

South Africa Police figures for 2002 – 3 also show high levels of crime. 60 South Africans are murdered each day, giving murder rates of 47.4 per 100 000 of the population. More than half of all murders were committed with firearms. Rape is at 115.3 per 100 000 although it is probably much higher since only one in three rape cases is reported to the police. Since 1983 at least 3049 policemen have been murdered. Despite some drops in crime rates over recent

76

years the fear of crime in South Africa is widespread. Data from the November 1999 Human Sciences Research Council National Opinion Survey showed 44% personally felt safe or very safe, whilst 47% felt 'unsafe' or 'very unsafe' (Humpries 2000:1; see also Baker 2008b:36).

Figures for Accra, Ghana, show similar large increases in the last few decades. Total crimes recorded by the police jumped from 26 946 in 1990 to 44 567 in 1996. Taking selected offences, murder rose from 20% per year to 51%, assault from 9551 to 17905 and theft from 7659 to 12911(Appiahene – Gyamfi 2003:170).

A 2001 Victimisation Survey in Kenya reported that 37% of Nairobi's residents had been victims of robbery, which 40% of the victims had been injured or killed as a result of violence used in the robbery. About 50% of the victims did not report their injury to the police because they felt it was a waste of time (UN – Habitat 2001).

There is no doubt that all the trends that are fast gaining ground in many African societies would require a different kind of policing altogether in order to contain the situation.

Nature of policing in post-colonial states

The mid-19th century ideology of policing that it was a public good and therefore deserved a state monopoly was largely unchallenged intellectually until the 1990s.It was regarded as self-evident that functions such as regulating society and maintaining order, preserving security, preventing crime, responding to crime and restoring order, and the use where necessary of instruments of coercion to assist in any of these matters for the state to undertake and the state alone.

Only in the state's hands it was argued could policing activities be required to be accountable, consistent and humane. In Africa, where the post-colonial state has always been much weaker that in the West, it is more common to have the public look up to and meet private security guards and CCTV operators at their workplace and in retail parks than the civil police.It is common to find local council wardens supervising vehicle parking and recreation areas and to anticipate protection in their street from electronic security and the neighbourhood watch more than civil police on the duty.

With an inefficient, invisible, corrupt and brutal police service the citizens never cease to provide their own local solutions and to their challenges initiate new forms with or without the approval of the state of dealing with the myriad problems that affect their wellbeing as a people.

In Africa as in the West it is common to see non state agencies engaged in street patrolling, guarding private and public property, order maintenance, arrest, search, detection, inspection and personal escort or protection.In fulfilling many of these duties they commonly bear firearms and other means of coercion, such as handcuffs, truncheons and pepper spray to, if necessary, enforce their activities.In other words, such policing groups do everything that the public police do and do it just as the police do it.Put in another way, law enforcement is a broader activity than simply what 'The Police do'.This is noted by Bayley and Shearing (2000) who argue that without close scrutiny it has become difficult to tell whether policing is being done by a government using sworn personnel, by an agent using a private security company, by a private security company using civilian employees, by a private company using public police or by a government employing civilians. The duo [Bayley and Shearing] further note that law enforcement in the last two decades (from the time of their publication) in developed and developing countries has been undergoing reconstruction, with not only a separation between those who authorise it from those who provide the service but a dispersal of both functions away from the state police or even away from the government.

Policing for business interests, residential communities cultural communities, individuals as well as the state is now provided by commercial security companies, formal voluntary non-governmental groups, individuals and even governments themselves as private suppliers of protection.

Policing is indeed viewed as a heterogeneous function undertaken by a plurality of providers using an array of techniques. This makes the government only one of the many contributors towards the security of citizens and their property. And, this explains why we have both public and private policing in many countries around the world. But given that the focus of this book is on policing by the government, there is need for us to understand the structure and organisation of the police force, in this case, in Zimbabwe which is the focus of the present chapter.

The Zimbabwe Republic Police (ZRP): Structure and Organisation

Until July 1980, the Zimbabwe Republic Police (ZRP) which is the national police force of Zimbabwe, was known as the British South Africa Police (BSAP). The police force of Zimbabwe comprises twelve departments namely; Administration, Boat Squadron, Canine Section, Criminal Investigations, Internal Security and Investigations (PISI), Police Air Wing, Police Support Unit, Riot Squad, Signals Branch, Special Constabulary, Uniformed Branch, and Women's Branch (Amnesty International 2005). In terms of number, the force has at least 39, 000 officers with its headquarters in the capital Harare at the Police General Headquarters (PGHQ) (The Military Balance 2003/2004).

The Zimbabwe police force is organised by province. It comprises uniformed national police namely, the Criminal Investigation Department and Traffic Police but with many other specialist support units such as Ceremonial, Canine, Riot Police, Police Internal Security and Intelligence Unit, and Paramilitary (Police Support Unit). The force has 17 known provinces which are headed by a Senior Assistant Commissioner General Augustine Chihuri, who exercise the overall command of the force. The Senior Assistant Commissioner General is deputised by four Deputy Commissioner Generals who form part of the Central Planning Committee (CPC) which is a decision passing board in the ZRP. The four Deputy Commissioner Generals are also deputised by five commissioners. This structure, thus, makes a Commissioner General, a five star General.

Zimbabwe Republic Police: Changes since 1980

By 1980, the force of the BSAP had a strength of about 9000 regular personnel, that is, black policemen and a further 25, 000 police reservists (nearly half of whom were white Zimbabweans of European ancestry). Considering the number of indigenous Zimbabweans and the fact that the country had now attained its national independence from the European settlers, there was need for an Africanisation of the police force including introducing many other changes.

With the advent of political independence so many changes took place in government institutions. The police force was not an exception. In the police force, those traditions that were only applicable to the white policemen during the colonial regime were introduced, starting with the advancement of the black policemen to senior positions including that of Police Commissioner. In 1982, for example, Mr Wiridzayi Nguruve, who had joined the police force in 1960 as a Constable, became the first black Commissioner of the force before he was succeeded by Mr Henry Mkurazhizha. Mkurazhizha was later succeeded by Mr Augustine Chihuri. These changes were meant to address the racial disparities that were created during the colonial regime and indeed now inherent in the government institutions, including the police force.

It should, however, be underlined that the changes in the police force after independence were not all that smooth as they met with some serious resistance. In fact, initially the black leadership in the Zimbabwean police force (now Zimbabwe Republic Police/ZRP) followed the philosophy of its predecessor, the BSAP. The police was still reactive and unaccountable till around 1985 when the police leadership under Commissioner Augustine Chihuri adopted a policing philosophy which emphasised public participation in affairs of the police.

As one of its major changes, the police force launched its first Service Charter in 1995 which emphasised service planning and public participation in affairs of the police and combating crime (ZBC News 12/04/2014). Through the Service Charter the police pronounced audibly its organisational and individual core values as well as service standards which define the minimum level of service that must be delivered to the community. This was an initiative and gesture to show that the police was now a people's force which would be guided by Corporate Governance principles. Some of the tenets the police adopted included transparency, accountability, efficient and effective use of resources, professionalism, co-operation with the public and quality service. To add on these, the ZRP has since the launch of its first Service Charter set up the Business Against Crime Committee, the Crime Consultative Committee, and Neighbourhood Watch Committees as part of incorporating the public in their initiative (ZBC News 12/03/2014).

The launching of the Service Charter by the ZRP was indeed the starting point of responsive and responsible policing by the black police in Zimbabwe: a complete shift from colonial policing to a more accountable and responsible policing of post-colonial Africa. The police was now expected to answer for the way they deliver and discharge their Constitutional Mandate. They were now answerable to the Stakeholders because they had realised from the mistakes of policing in colonial times that the business of managing crime is not for the police alone.

The other major change in the police force after independence was the introduction of women in the force which was meant to move along with time in the new millennium and to cater of the needs and interests of women in society. Before independence, very few women had place in the police force as the force was highly considered as a job not fit for either children or women. From his researches Cohn (1978: 198) observed that:

Many male officers believe that women will not be able to handle violent encounters nor provide adequate assistance to male partners, that they will be injured more easily, or use firearms excessively. The male officers also contend that the women will not be aggressive enough to assert themselves at critical moments nor authoritative enough to command respect from the community.

According to Cohn (1978:197), 'more bluntly, Dallas, Chief Don Byrd was quoted in the same post article as remarking: If you put two women together [in a squad] they fight. If you put male and female together, they fornicate.' To him, women were not employable within the forces. They were a baggage that would be too heavy for the organisation. Engaging women was for those that were not serious with pursuing with the ideals of the organisation but objects of passion, thus no serious commander would deploy women hoping they would yield results, unless may be it is about typing a couple of documents or to file them.

Consistent with Security Council resolution 1820 and 1325, the police force now has a place for women. In Zimbabwe as in many parts of the world, the resistance to use women officers has broken down. There is wide understanding now that women officers are equally as effective as their male counterparts. They have proved beyond any shade of doubt that no task is too insurmountable, no task is unachievable. In most police forces today many women have ascended to high leadership positions.

The level of intellect of women according to many researchers is in no way inferior to that of the men. Given a chance women have been to contribute to the development of their economies in a very big way. Women are not second class citizens, thus they have to be accorded the same opportunities as men.For organisations that have taken aboard the philosophy that women are employable after all, they have deployed them to administrative duties or such menial tasks while the challenging tasks have been assigned to the masculine gender.

There are so many situations in the work environment that need the women folk for results to be achieved. In the absence of female officers, many women suspects, accused have been violated by male officers in a manner that is so bad. Where men have feared such allegations of abuse they

83

have for example in border patrols left women suspects unsearched. They have thus made such women escape with their loot of precious minerals hid in their under garments, causing the economy to severely bleed in the process.

Women police officers in the majority of cases have an extraordinary understanding of issues to deal with women and children. Women have a soft spot in their hearts that shows empathy, passion and kindness. In this vein women would do exceptionally well in:

- Victim Friendly Offices
- Prosecution duties
- Roadblocks

Following this world wide understanding that women officers are as competent, the SARPCCO Chiefs endorsed the launch of a Women's Network for the police officers in the region to show their unparalleled support for the cause of women. This Women's Network is guided by the following objectives:

- To encourage women in sport and recreation
- Poverty alleviation
- Resource mobilisation
- Equal job opportunities
- Training and development.

This initiative is thus expected to acknowledge the fact that women are equal partners not objects of abuse at workplaces.

Yet, as already been underscored, during the colonial era in Africa (as in the case of Zimbabwe) very few women were recruited into the Police force. When they were engaged they were attached to administration duties or any other menialtasks in the force that did not require high rated skills. This included cooking and cleaning in the police camps. The introduction of women as full-fledged members of the force in post-colonial Zimbabwe, is therefore, not a mean achievement for both women and the country in general. It is a clear testimony that contemporary Zimbabwean policing has managed to traverse the gender disparities in the society which was largely a result of the colonial regime's patriarchal organisation. Women officers can now be seen on all ranks in the police service. This has improved the face of policing in Zimbabwe as elsewhere on the continent since women officers are very good if not exceptional in crimes of passion such as rape of adults, and juveniles and domestic violence cases.

This is also consistent with the views by Kofi Annan (2002) who noted that there is no way the Millennium Development Goals (MDGs) can be achieved without the involvement of women themselves. As anyone can testify, women are central in the development discourse, the police included.Many women police officers are now visible even on United Nations Peacekeeping duties across Africa and elsewhere.

Besides, contemporary policing in Zimbabwe as elsewhere in the world is now emphasising the concept of human rights. During the colonial era, the police force was so brutal as though they were not aware of the United Nations Human Rights Charter (UNHRC). The police was the law unto themselves as they were invincible and ultimate.According to Crashaw (1999), in a democratic state where the rule of law prevails no person or institution is above the law. The police is, thus,now expected to work entirely and always within the confines of law. It is in full recognition of this facet that the Zimbabwe Republic Police has engraved this aspect among its individual core values.

As human rights are protected by law, this means that the law protecting human rights must be respected and obeyed in the course of every police activity (see Crashaw 1999). The police are thus expected to operate within the four corners of the limits prescribed by law. Any other powers used by the police that violate law will be condemned as *'ultra vires'*.This clearly shows that policing in post-colonial Africa, and Zimbabwe in particular, has now and is becoming even more responsive and sensitive to the needs of the people the police themselves are part. When it is inevitable to break or bend the laws the police has to justify such actions. At times the police have to use force and other means to prevent or detect crimes, maintain or restore public order but such force must be limited in scope to that activity and no more (Crashaw 1999).

The other major development that occurred in post-colonial policing in Zimbabwe is community policing which introduced a number of policing programmes such as:

Community Relations Scheme

In an enduring effort to improve the image of the police as well as public relations the ZRP embarkedin educating members of the public on the centrality of their participation in working with the police. It was from this background that the community relations officers were appointed, so that the police would now 'participate in all the massactivities from grassroots to national level,' according to Muzenda (1998:18). This thus saw in March 1986 ten Community Relations Liaison Officers (CRLOs) posts being established in the Harare South District, mostly in the high-density suburbs of Mbare, Warren Park and Marimba Park. The pilot project started in these areas because firstly most domestic violence cases reported to the police came from these areas. Secondly, it was because the police and the public relationships were very tense in these areas.

Through this organ, the ZRP started working with other agencies such as Musasa Project, Legal and Clinic, Shelter Trust, Connect, among others.

The CRLOnow became overwhelmed with clients who required counselling services. The skills of these officers were further enhanced by Connect with the first group of CRLOs having begun the Systematic Counseling Course in June 1989.

In a nutshell the CRLOs were tasked with the following specific roles:

- Spearheading education and crime awareness campaigns in their respective communities.
- Reinforcing police/community liaison where it had broken down.
- Creating fora interactions where they never existed before.
- Improving dialogue with the community where relations might have been strained.
- Sustaining good relations between the police and the community.
- Providing counseling services to victims of crime.

It should be underscored that this scheme has certainly paid dividends in as far as bringing the much-sought rapport between the police and the public. The police are no longer viewed with suspicion or as enemies but as partners in crime management. They also can now depend on assistance from the people, for example, bicycles to Avondale, computers to

Dzivarasekwa, motor vehicle to Borrowdale, sponsorship to the Police Staff College, etc.

Police Constabulary Scheme

The coming aboard of this meant to encourage the public to be unquestionably active in crime control. The branch is in 3 distinct categories, viz Branch A, B and C.

Neighbourhood Watch Committee (NWC)

This is a community based activity supported by the local police which is aimed at pursuing effective crime prevention. It calls for all property owners to be visible and responsive so as to ensure the protection of their own property and that of their neighbours. The approach can assume various forms that include the marking of property, reporting any suspicious activities, patrolling the neighbourhood and making frantic efforts to improve or upgrade the security of their homes. If the property owners work together such neighbourhood will be a 'no go area' to criminals. The NWCs develop their own patrolling programmes and crime prevention initiatives. When they go on patrol the NWC should however be in the company of one regular police officer. This officer helps to explain the law so that the NWCs will not take the law into their own hands. Where this initiative has been employed the communities have witnessed a significant drop in crime. The NWCs are however faced with some challenges, chief of which is shortage of basic equipment, uniforms, transport and so forth.

Air Wing

Up to 2002 the air wing consisted of 60 pilots who were and with some still members of the Police Constabulary and share between them 20 aircraft. The aircraft were supposed to be always on standby in different regions of the country ready to come in with the assistance sought. They were used in emergencies to transport personnel and material from one place to another, to track car thieves, cattle rustlers and patrol boarders. This scheme is indeed one of the oldest community policing initiatives dating back to the 1940s. To qualify for membership one had to be a pilot and an aircraft owner. This programme has almost died because of the current sad political challenges the country is facing. The majority of the members in this programme were white commercial farmers whose farms were repossessed by the state for redistribution. In cases of emergencies the ZRP is now being assisted by the Air Force of Zimbabwe.

Suggestion Boxes and Hotlines

As a way to reaching out and improving community meaningful participation in policing and flow of timely and relevant information from the public the police embarked on the use of suggestion boxes and hotlines. The advantage of this strategy was that of anonymity. The strategy has promised to yield good results though malcontents in some communities continue to vandalise these boxes or call on the hotlines to shout abuses or raise false alarm.

Construction of Bases, Posts or Satellites

In order to redress the colonial legacy which saw police stations located far away from the black majority (Norton, for example), bases posts and satellites were constructed, and many such efforts are still being pursued. The focus of this initiative is to increase the response time to reports in accordance with the stated standard response times in the Service Plan. The Service Plan is basically a working document of the police which details how the police will pursue their mandate.

Crime Consultative Committees

These have been formed to create a forum for sharing information and formulation of crime fighting strategies between the police and the public. The forum helps the parties to clear any grey areas and justify any positions adopted so as to create effective synergies. The committee must be selected in a transparent manner, so that it is not aligned to particular groupings within that community. This would polarize its position which ought to be discouraged for the effective survival of such committees.

Police Junior Call

The strategy here is to 'catch them young' as a way of building disciplined citizens who shun ill-gotten benefits. The children are kept off the streets so that they are preoccupied by positive police programmes. This would also help create a sound recruitment base for a future force.

Business against Crime Initiatives

This is an initiative that challenges the captains of industry and commerce to join hands with the community in the fight against crime. These fora would allow a diffusion of constructive ideas, programmes or initiatives between the police and the business world to curb the upsurge in white-collar crime which has almost ravaged the business terrain. The initiative would allow for the flow of resources from the companies to the aid of the police.

Home Officer Scheme

Is the latest community policing initiative which is characterised by subdivisions of the area which a station is responsible for into small and manageable geographical portions where an officer and sometimes a group of officers are assigned for long periods to perform a majority of their policing activities.

The officer(s) attached to an area are charged with the ultimate responsibility of getting as much detail about the area as is possible. The officers actually cultivate a working relationship with the residents so as to design enduring strategies in the fight against crime in the area.

Among several other initiatives the home officers shall be responsible for:

- Introducing suggestion boxes in their areas to bolster flawless communication.
- Investigating the cases reported in this area.
- Providing counseling services to members of this community.
- Assisting with background checks for aspiring police applicants.
- Remarketing of the Service Charter.
- Attending crime management meetings in the area (see Service Charter 1995 2013).

More so, policing in post-colonial Zimbabweas elsewhere in post-colonial Africa is now emphasising ethics, what is now commonly known as ethical policing. This is not to say that police is never faced with certain dilemmas where ethical behaviour is concerned. Ordinarily, the craft and profession of policing is extremely demanding, physically, emotionally and intellectually such that making decisions where ethical questions arise is sometimes challenging. Crawshaw (1999) summarises it all when he notes that the Police Officials are normally exposed to:

➤ The effects of serious criminality on victims;

➤ The frustrations of being unable to deliver the perpetrators of very serious crime to justice;

➤ Personal danger and discomfort;

➤ Pressure from community, the news media, and politicians to obtain results.

The challenges that the police have to contain with in this regard include but not limited to the following code: Citizenry served by law enforcement officials with protection of all their rights and interests. This code of conduct has eight articles which are:

Article 1: requires all law enforcement officials to fulfil the duty imposed on them by law;

Article 2: requires law enforcement officials to respect and protect human dignity and maintain and uphold human rights;

Article 3: requires law enforcement officials to use force only when strictly necessary and to the extent required for the performance of their duty;

Article 4: requires law enforcement officials to maintain confidentiality of matters of a confidential nature which come into their possession;

Article 5: reasserts the absolute prohibition of torture or ill-treatment;

Article 6: requires law enforcement officials to ensure the full protection of the health of persons detained in custody;

Article 7: prohibits law enforcement officials from committing any act of corruption;

Article 8: requires law enforcement officials to respect the law and the Code of Conduct and to prevent and rigorously oppose any violations of them.

Worth noting as a positive development in post-colonial Africa, and Zimbabwe in particular, also includes the emphasising of the philosophy of good policing that involves not only community participation but ethics in its practice. According to Crawshaw (1999), the basic elements of good policing in a democracy are policing which encompasses the following:

Respectful of the law
➢ Unlawful and arbitrary policing undermines the rule of law.

Respectful of human rights
➢ Human rights are meant to protect individuals and groups of people from abuse of power by the state. It is thus essential for the police and other security organs to understand that human rights are entitlements and not privileges granted by a government. The police and indeed other security organs must understand also that human rights are inalienable (cannot be taken away) and inherent in every human being and that they are not a series of obstacles which somehow have to be overcome, circumvented or ignored during the processes of policing in contemporary societies.

Respectful of Democratic Principles
➢ It is important for the police to understand that accountability and participation are the pillars to good governance.

Humane and ethical
➢ The police must endeavour to assist those in need.

Effective
➢ The police must indeed provide security to its community.

While police could use firearms during the colonial era, in post-colonial Africa Zimbabwe as elsewhere in Africa, the use of firearms is strictly regulated mainly due to the respect and upholding of human rights. Governments are ensuring that arbitrary or abusive use of force and firearms by police officials is severely punished as a criminal offence according to the law [Principle 7 of the Universal Declaration of Human Rights].

And, while those in police custody were always at the mercy of the arresting officers,in post-colonial Africa, persons in police custody have rights that must be observed and respected by everyone including the members of the police force. In terms of the 2013 Constitution of Zimbabwe Section 50, the rights of the arrested or detained persons are clearly spelt-out. The details in the aforementioned section is supported by Article 9 of the Universal Declaration of Human Rights (UDHR)which states that no one shall be subjected to arbitrary arrest, detention or exile.

In short, the advent of political independence in Zimbabwe as in many other independent African countries witnessed a shift in the policing philosophy. The pre-independence policing initiatives were no longer relevant as independence meant that all people were now equal: no race was still more important than the other. This allowed for equal opportunities, fairness, and equity across the political and colour divide.

The brutality, coercion, and segregation that characterised the policing of pre-independence era disappeared into oblivion as the Union Jack was lowered and handed over to Prince Charles. Colour was no longer significant in influencing policies and programmes in independent Zimbabwe. All Zimbabweans were now equal in virtually all respects, at least in principle. The previous view that defined the police as an enemy of the people was as well buried with the coming of political independence. The police in independent Zimbabwe, thus, had the obligation to commit themselves and earnestly determined to correct the perceptions that the people previously had, particularly the majority black who had suffered at the hands of the brutality of the colonial police force.

The police were now guided in their operations by Section 93(1) of the Constitution of Zimbabwe. This section has now been amended by Amendment Number 20 and the Police Service is now a creation of Section 219 of the Constitution of Zimbabwe which provides that there is a Police Service which is responsible for:

a) Detecting, investigating and preventing crime;

b) Preserving the internal security of Zimbabwe;

c) Protecting and Securing the lives and property of the people;

d) Maintaining law and order;

e) Upholding the Constitution and enforcing the law without fear of favour with such other bodies as may be established by the law for the purpose.

Accordingly, no person is more Zimbabwean than the other. Similarly, no individual has more rights than any other person as in terms of the Human Rights Charter. This is because at independence, the hostility that prevailed during the colonial era was dealt with a blow as it was defined as evil for indeed it was, perpetuated by a system bent on advancing the egocentric and nefarious interests of the minority.

To show that the police in Zimbabwe was now moving towards being a people's force that emphasises sanity, equality of all regardless of race, religion, and ethnic group, it recruited to its memberships from the belligerent forces, that is the Rhodesian police, ZANLA and ZIPRA Cadres (Police Museum – Morris Depot).This was meant to reflect the new realities of the independence that had come following heavy fighting within the country as well as neighbouring countries. This fighting left so many dead, maimed, orphaned and the surviving populace would surely need a people's force that is responsive, accountable, and sensitive to their concerns.

Thus, the thrust of the new policing philosophy was meant to make the police and public enduring partners, partners that would be there for each other honestly and in earnest. This was derived from a statement by the then Prime Minister of Zimbabwe, Robert Mugabe on the 13th March of 1985 who said:

We must underscore the point that effective policing must derive from and flourishing on the good will and cooperation with the whole community from whom any police force derives its legitimacy.

In driving this notion, the police started drawing up initiatives to ease the tense atmosphere that existed between the force and the public.The nation started to witness the birth of satellite tents for close accessibility, introduction of the neighbourhood watch committees and networking with other agencies such as legal Aid, Musasa Project, Marriage Guidance. The office of the Community Relations Liaison Officer was also introduced so that it would be the vehicle between the police and the people.

Chapter Five

Criminal Justice System in Zimbabwe: The Police and Citizens' Responsibility, Accountability and Compliance

Gabriel Chevallier, writing in 1936, once said: 'The law, as manipulated by clever and highly respected rascals, still remains the best avenue for a career of honourable and leisurely plunder'.

While Chevallier directed his writing to those in the legal profession, the writing could also be applied to those involved in criminal justice such as members of the police force. Criminal justice is the system of practices and institutions of governments directed at upholding social control, deterring and mitigating crime or sanctioning those who violate laws with criminal penalties and rehabilitation efforts (Samuel 1992).

The president's Commission on Law Enforcement and Administration of Justice (CLEAJ) defined criminal justice system as the means for society to enforce the standards of conduct necessary to protect individuals and the community (CLEAJ 1967). In Canada, the criminal justice system aims to balance the goals of crime control and prevention, and justice (equality, fairness, protection of individual rights) (see Schmolka n.d.).

In England, the criminal justice system aims to reduce crime by bringing more offences to justice, and to raise public confidence that the system is fair and will deliver for the law-abiding citizen (see Criminal Justice 1995). In China, the criminal justice system aims to keep the society function well and protect every person's right (Wan Peng 2013). In

Sweden, the overall goal for the criminal justice system is to reduce crime and increase the security of the people (see Criminal Justice, Scottish 1995). In Zimbabwe, the overarching goal for criminal justice system is to protect all citizens and ensure peace and order in society.

As could be seen from the overall goal for criminal justice system in all the aforementioned countries, justice has the duty to enforce law and maintain order in society. On this note, it should be clear that criminal justice system consists of three main agencies namely; legislative (responsible for creating laws), adjudication (responsible for trial and judgement of cases in courts of law), and corrections (jails, prisons,probation, and parole). Yet these three distinct agencies operate together both under the rule of law and as the principal means of maintaining the rule of law in society (Walker 1992).

Besides, it is worth noting that the first contact a defendant has with the criminal justice system is usually with the police who investigate the suspected wrongdoing and make an arrest but if the suspect is dangerous to the whole nation, a national law enforcement agency is called in. This means that a police is a person empowered by the state to enforce the law, protect property, and limit civil disorder. When warranted, police officers or law enforcement agencies are empowered to use force and other forms of legal coercion and means to effect public and social order (Policy Studies Institute [n.d.]; Harper 2000).

Yet, it is widely published that many police forces around the world (Zimbabwe included) suffer from police corruption to either a greater or lesser degree regardless of the fact that police force is usually a public sector service paid through taxes (see Harper 2000; Mackey 1997; Newburn 1999; BBC 8/02/2010). By police corruption, we mean a form of police

98

misconduct in which law enforcement officers break their social contract and abuse their power for personal or department gain. These include, but not limited to:

(i) Soliciting or accepting bribes in exchange for not reporting an illegal activity or to overlook a crime or possible future crime.

(ii) Flouting the police code of conduct in order to secure convictions of suspects, for instance, through the use of falsified evidence.

(iii) Participating deliberately and systematically, in organised crime activities themselves.

(iv) Fixing: When police officers undermine criminal prosecutions by withholding evidence or failing to appear at judicial hearings, for bribery or as a personal favour.

(v) Perjury: When police officers lie to protect other officers or oneself in a court of law or a department investigation.

(vi) Ticket fixing: When police officers cancel traffic tickets as a favour to their friends and family of other police officers.

(vii) Internal payoffs: When police officers or prerogatives and perquisites of law enforcement organisations such as shifts and holidays, being bought and sold.

(viii) Shakedowns: When police officers steal items for personal use from a crime scene or an arrest. This can be classified under theft and burglary.

(ix) Corruption of authority: When police officers receive free drinks, meals and other gratuities because they are police officers. Whether intentionally or unintentionally, such gratuities convey an image of corruption (see Newburn 1999).

Yet, as soon as we are confronted with this reality, Gabriel Chevallier's (1996) assertion highlighted in the introduction of this chapter, comes into mind. The question that boggles the minds of the public, who in this case are tax payers – the source of the salaries for police officers – is: 'Does Chevallier's assertion apply to our Zimbabwean police officers? We hope not, but we suspect that in some respects, greater or lesser, it does apply to the Zimbabwean police officers commonly known as Zimbabwe Republic Police (ZRP). This suspicion calls for the need for the ZRP to engage in self-introspection, to examine its role in order to move along with time in the force's quest to promote peace, security and order in the country. The members of ZRP need to examine their own lives and that of their profession. As Socrates once proclaimed 'an unexamined life is not worth living.' But as we will demonstrate in this chapter, the ZRP, though perhaps not all of its members are already falling behind the new times in which we live,exhibit the highest level of moral probity and professionalism possible.

To substantiate this claim, we quote a number of cases, alleged or confirmed where some police officers in the ZRP, have, over the years been involved in some form of corrupt activities and other such illicit dealings:

Box 1: In the Sunday Mail story of March 27, 2015, was a headline "Traffic cops destroy spot fine documents" by Itai Mazire. In the story, Mazire reports that officers at Featherstone, Chivhu, Shamva, Bindura Rural and Central, and Kwekwe Central Police Stations destroyed z69j documents, which are the source records on fines issued. In all 5033 pages of documentation disappeared. In her 2013 report, Controller and Auditor-General, Mrs Mildred Chiri reveals disturbing details of discrepancies on spot fines. She could not rule out fraudulent activities by Police Officers manning roadblocks who charged different amounts in spot fines for similar offences. According to Chiri, audit carried out by her department revealed that 'there were inconsistencies in charges levied against motorists. Some were below and others above the standard charges in the deposit fines schedule for offences without any satisfactory reasons [...] Police records showed three incidences in Victoria Falls where the officers handed down spot fines to motorists which are not reflected in the deposit fines schedule [...] Victoria Falls Traffic Police charged [a motorist] for not having a plate light and was ordered to pay US$ 20 but the spot fine for the traffic offence in the deposit fines schedule is US$ 5. Another motorist was charged US$ 10 for failing to be secured in a seat belt but the charge is US $5. Hwange Police undercharged a motorist after recording a fine of US$ 15 instead of US$ 20 for driving without licence.'

Box 2: In the Team Zimbabwe story of 26 March 2014 was a headline "Drama as corrupt Police Officers are arrested at a roadblock" written by Bhebhe Mandla. The story reports that the Police Officers had 'barricaded' Khami Road causing commuter omnibus operators to flee to Luveve Road in Bulawayo. Onlookers said they had a hilarious time watching Police Officers running away throwing away the money they had been paid as a bribe in a bid to obliterate incriminating evidence. Kombi drivers who were reached for comment disclosed that the anti-corruption unit arrived in a combi and in plain clothes fooling the Policemen, who had set up a roadblock at the flyover to believe they were regular drivers who would pay a bribe to pass the roadblock. The Police Officers then stopped the kombi and were given $2 after demanding a bribe. As soon as one of the officers pocketed the money, they flashed their badges and told him he was under arrest. Realising they were in hot-soup, the other officers at the roadblock took to their heels emptying their pockets of money in the process.

Box 3: In the Standard Newspaper (1 December 2013) appeared the headline "Zimbabwe Police Force needs serious reformation" by Kimion Tagwirei. In the story, Tagwirei claims that the general mandate of the police – enforcing the law, security, peace and order – has been gradually fading as the law enforcers dramatically turned to opportunists and corrupt money-mongers. It has become public knowledge that the Zimbabwe Police is turning roadblocks into money-spinning ventures, worsening most people's mistrust of them [...]. Not only on the roads where their corruption now seems normal to many; but in almost all areas. Where one or two officers deal with a case, they can safely change goal posts, demand bribes and release criminals. We have resultantly come to a point where the rich live above the law, while the poor succumb to any corrupt machinations in Zimbabwe [...] Many people just fear the famous police cliché – "I can arrest you [...]" So, people find no better option than paying bribes. In Zimbabwe, the police usually demand bribes, indirectly or directly depending on the situation. This leaves the innocent and helpless ordinary men questioning "Who shall police the Police?"The ZRP as a whole is undeniably one of the most corrupt situations regionally [...] Our government must formulate and implement mechanisms that will deal with institutionalised corruption at all levels.

Box 4: In the Zim Eye story of 7 January 2013 by Chris Tongogara was a headline "Zimbabwe: Over 100 ZRP Officers blacklisted for corruption". In the story, Tongogara reports that 'the ZRP Officer commanding Harare Province, Clemence Munoriyarwa confirmed yesterday that over a hundred police officers had been reported and cited for corruption. He spoke to hundreds of officers and other delegates who gathered in Highfields, Harare for a Police Service Charter re-launch as he reiterated that it was ideal that Police re-ignite the confidence and trust that they once carried among public members. The escalating complaints registered against the Police had triggered a serious review on Police professionalism and conduct [...]'. Tongogara added that 'the arm of corruption had mainly derailed public confidence in Police Service and it was about time the Police returned to the principles stated on the Service Charter and serve the public in a professional capacity through executing proper police duties and functions [....]. Thousands of corruption complaints especially by road traffic Police reach the senior Police Officers daily from the public [...]. In 2012, 103 Police officers were arrested for corruption'.

Box 5: In the Nehanda Radio story of 8 March 2013 was a headline "Video: Zimbabwe Traffic Police caught on camera accepting US$ 20 bribe to avoid a speeding ticket." The story reports that in the film, the biker who was doing 81 km per hour in a 60 km zone, was asked to pay a US$ 20. The Police accepted the money unaware that they were being secretly filmed.

Box 6: In the Zimbabwe Situation story of 11 November 2013 was a headline "Chihuri blames poor pay for ZRP sleaze" by ZimsitRep. In the story, ZimsitRep reports that ZRP Chief, Augustine Chihuri has urged the government to address working conditions for the Police and suggested that poor salaries were encouraging vice in the organisation. Junior Police Officers are notorious for demanding bribes, especially from motorists, but the ZRP was recently forced to admit that the rot also affected its top ranks. Addressing a senior officers' Conference in Harare last week (a week before the publication of this story), Chihuri said '[...]conditions of services, particularly salaries and accommodation, are at the centre of hardships faced by Police Officers. I am not at all trying to justify corruption and those who are corrupt will surely face stiff punishment, but some of the situations are dire and provoke corrupt tendencies'.

Box 7: In a case recorded: Case S v Machinya & Ors S-42-91, three policemen in plain clothes saw a man carrying a small stove, immediately suspected him of theft, punched him, refused to listen to his explanation, handcuffed him, threw him to the ground, kicked him several times on the face and body, then marched him to the station and threw him into the cells for the night. He had offered no provocation or resistance and was completely innocent. His eye haemorrhaged and his jaw was fractured by 'the worst type of gang bullying and gratuitous violence under the cloak of authority'. The deterrent aspect of sentence and interests of the public were of paramount importance, overriding personal considerations. The loss of employment and benefits by these long-serving policemen was no consequence as they were quite unfitted to the post. The sentence on each of the three policemen was 15 months imprisonment, of which six were suspended, was confirmed for assault with intent to do grievous bodily harm.

Source: Feltoe 1998: 42

Box 8: In a case recorded: Case S v Manhivi & Ors S-30-91, the judge pronounced that brutality by the police in investigating crime and interrogating suspects must be punished effectively and a fine will be wholly inadequate, save in exceptional circumstances. Even if retribution is no longer regarded as a legitimate object of punishment, the humiliating and shameful treatment and the need for a deterrent sentence justified the sentence.

Three policemen had struck repeated blows with their fists and a ruler to the shoulders, back and face of a female suspect, causing bruises and some bleeding. A twelve-month prison sentence, with half suspended was confirmed on appeal.

Source: Feltoe 1998: 42

> **Box 9:** In a case recorded: Case S v Chipere S-201-92, a plainclothes policeman declined to identify himself but forcibly arrested complainant for suspected drinking in public, felling him and then stabbing him on the forehead with a spear and then again on his hand as he tried to protect his chest from injury. The facial wound required 3 stitches. The complainant was entitled to challenge his authority; and the policeman had used more force than was necessary to secure the arrest.
>
> The judge, on passing sentence on the policeman, pronounced that the assaults by law enforcement agents on ordinary people in the execution of their duties must be deterred to prevent animosity arising between them and the citizenry. Custodial sentences will almost invariably be imposed, unless there are exceptional mitigatory factors. The Supreme Court confirmed the sentence of 8 months' imprisonment, of which 3 were suspended for assault with intent to do grievous bodily harm in the course of duty by police.
>
> *Source: Feltoe 1998: 42*

While prevalence of police corruption in Zimbabwe, as elsewhere on the continent and beyond, is allegedly high, it is hard to come by given that the corrupt activities tend to happen in secret yet police organisations in the country have little incentive to publish information about corruption (see also Kutjak Ivkovic 2003; Skolnick 2002). For this reason, police officials and researchers alike have argued that in some countries, large scale corruption involving the police not only exists but can even become institutionalised (Kratcoski 2002). For example, one study of corruption in the Los Angeles Police Department focusing particularly on the Rampart Scandal proposed that certain forms of police corruption may be the norm, rather than the exception, in American policing (Grant 2003).

In another case in the United Kingdom in 2002 in which internal investigations were launched into the largest police force, the Metropolitan Police, Operation Tiberius found that the force was so corrupt that organised criminals were able to infiltrate Scotland Yard "at will" by bribing corrupt officers and that Britain's biggest force suffered endemic corruption at the time (Harper 2014).

In Zimbabwe, the cases cited in the boxes 1-6 suggest that the ZRP is not an exception when it comes to corrupt activities and other such illicit dealings. Yet where corruption exists, the widespread existence of a Blue Code of Silence among the police can prevent the corruption from coming to light. Blue Code of Silence, also known as Blue Wall of Silence, Blue Code, and Blue Shield, are terms used in the U.S to denote the unwritten rule that exists among police officers not to report on a colleague's errors, misconducts or crime but claim ignorant of such activities (Mullen 2000; Quint and Giacomazzi Andrew 2010). As pointed out by Jerome Skolnick (2002), officers in these situations commonly fail to report corrupt activities or choose to provide false testimony to outside investigators just to cover up criminal activities by their fellow officers.

What handicaps police delivery in contemporary society in many African countries?

In recent years the media, electronic and otherwise has been awash with reports of acts of gross indiscipline and corrupt activities by police officers of all ranks and files. This has been a saddening development in the history of the police and a lot of concern has been raised. Many people have been asking why indiscipline has gone to such levels in the forces.

In the majority of cases the following reasons have been cited as the causes of such deplorable acts and behaviours:

Economic environment
- Shortage of uniforms
- Lack of fuel
- Lack of reliable vehicles
- Lack of reliable equipment such as radio equipment, public order and subaqua equipment
- Lack of stationery
- Inadequate training of officers
- Inadequate human resource base
- Poor remuneration
- Poor accommodation
- Low promotional prospects

Political environment
- Polarisation of society
- Poor leadership
- Political clashes
- Political interference
- Political decisions
- Interference of NGOs in the internal affairs of a state
- Civic society campaigns to destabilise state

Social environment
- Social fabric no more
- Moral decadence now rifle
- Absence of respect of life
- Corrupt society
- Hustle with public

Technical environment

- High network of criminal activity
- So many crimes coming with technology particularly in the banking sector
- Criminal intelligence moving much faster than police intelligence

Legal environment
- Legal system has not been complementing the effort of the police in recent years.
- Bail in undeserving decisions
- Corruption influencing decisions
- Legal provisions not moving fast enough with the trend of crime
- Lawyers defending criminals for financial gains such that in the end criminals get away with crime

Operational Challenges
- Lack of motivation on employees
- Leaking of 'operational objective' to the subject of the operation, for example, a raid on gold panners may be leaked by those with interests there.
- Unclear operational guidelines

These and many other such problems associated with police force have over the years compromised the quality of delivery by the police to the extent that many now believe that (the cops are never there when you need them' (Cohn 1978:10).

Yet, after all this has been said and done, a question that remains lingering in the minds of many is: 'How these challenges could be addressed even in the face of the economic problems that many African countries such as

Zimbabwe are currently experiencing?' The next chapter tries to shed more light on this and other such questions.

Chapter Six

Policing, ethics, and corporate governance: Policing in a changing society

As we have demonstrated earlier in this book, Chavallier's assertion does apply, in some respects, to the Zimbabwe Republic Police (ZRP). Basing on our findings, we claim that the Zimbabwe Republic Police is already falling behind the new times in which we live. In this chapter, we propose some thoughts as to how the police profession could possibly meet the challenges of the new millennium and strive to foster a peaceful and orderly society bolstered by corporate governance and community policing.

Community policing, ethics, and corporate governance

The world-over, so many public institutions are overwhelmingly riddled with the problem of unethical conduct from public officials. This evil has permeated virtually all ranks and files of organisations in society, the police included.It requires the involvement of all societal members and good ethics to effectively deal with the evil. In the next sections we discuss how community policing and ethics as incorporated in corporate governance could be handy in promoting good and effective policing.

Community policing
Traditionally people used to be responsible for their own safety, wellbeing and protection. Each individual had a sole obligation to ensure that his possessions, interests and family were secure. Society was thus a jungle were each man fought

111

his own war, each man stood for himself and his immediate family. This was not functional and as society evolved better thinking crept in and policing was conceived, nurtured and brought forth as the only remedy to the plethora of challenges man had to contain with his endeavour to survive effectively and sustainably.

Trojanowicz and Bucqueroux (1994) define community policing as a philosophy and organisational strategy that promotes a new partnership between the people and the police. As noted by Trojanowicz and Dixon (1974), such an understanding of policing implies that once the community and police develop a working relationship, both parties can engage in the goal sharing and, as a result, form productive working relationship. This sums Trojanowicz and Bucqueroux's (1990) argument that through community policing the police and community can work together to solve such problems as crime, fear of crime, social and physical disorder, and neighbourhood decay given that community policing shifts the way traditional police departments used to operate by decentralising the rank and file by allowing police officers to work hand in hand with members of the community. Peak (1997) shares the same view of policing when he argues that policing emerged as the dominant direction of thinking in crime prevention, which unifies the police and the community. This entails that the police in Zimbabwe, as elsewhere around the world, would and should now assume the responsibility of ensuring the uncontested safety and serenity of man. In fact, as society continues to grow and develop, the police should now go beyond the provision of law and order alone but do a host of things for man to show that man cannot live wholesomely without the police by his side.

We should underline that society especially in formerly colonised countries has, over the years, not taken the police seriously due to a number of reasons. In some cases, society has taken police as a bicycle that is only required when one has reason to ride on it. As soon as s/he has achieved his objective s/he soon forgets the role of the bicycle in his life. They forget that police is part and parcel of the society that should live with them now and forever considering the imperfection of human nature.

Society is an aggregation of individuals converging from a diversity of backgrounds and this naturally yields conflict and in the natural no two minds think alike thus it is a goose chase to believe that society would last a minute without the police.

We underline that the minds of the people constantly need to be guided, reminded of rules and regulations governing good order. Left to itself the world would turn upside down. Naturally people cannot relate to each other in a way Jesus taught 'to love thy neighbour, to be the brothers' keeper'.People always find reason to go contrary to the teachings that promote the spirit of brotherhood. This is largely so because man is in persistent competition with his environment and himself, and it seems he will not tire and give up. It is for this reason why people abandoned the state of nature as propounded by Tomas Hobbes: they had realised that man by nature is selfish and egoistic that if left unchecked could nothing other than promoting his own interests and desires. This is also the reason why sophisticated machines were manufactured to deal precisely with humans and not animals. To this end, the police are an essential component of society that makes things happen in a manner that is progressive. To this Cohn (1978:15) says: 'no one is advocating that we do away with policing. The problem is one of defining what it is we want and how what we want is to be implemented effectively, meaningfully, democratically and fairly'.

The police remain an integral component of any society, developed or underdeveloped. No society has citizens that are all upright. Even out of only twelve disciples Jesus had, not all the twelve shared the same vision with him. Society is, thus, bound to see fighting all the time in pursuit of ends that would bring gratification to the individuals.

We argue that man left to himself would not only hurt himself but others around him. Even Satan who was also commanding a third of angels in heaven failed to obey God's law. And, if angels can be fallible what about fallible human beings? This means that only a society that leaves its members unto themselves can only risk yielding chaos and nothing else better.Thus, as for human societies, no society should risk by allowing man to govern himself. He would hurt himself and others. The police have to provide the corrective role through all seasons to ensure peace prevails. Where there is peace, citizens work progressively for the uplifting of their economies and social status.

Even with the police it is difficult to contain or deal with crime. To this John Anderson (1979:5) argues: 'at all events police should be aware that to pursue the elimination of crime is to lay a false trail but that to regulate its incidence within tolerable levels is the aim of democratic policing'.

Crime elimination is not a practical possibility or reality. Resources the world over are scarce and their allocation will always create disparities that present opportunities for discontent. This would inevitably lead to crime of one form or other. Dealing with crime requires a systems approach to policing as the one shown in fig 3 below:

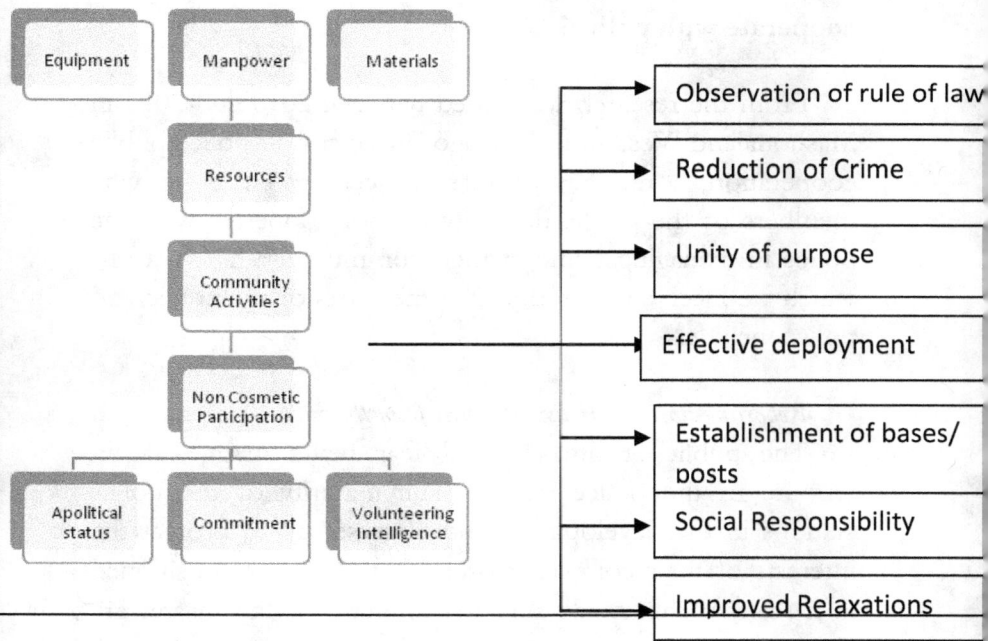

Equipment	Manpower	Materials

Resources

Community Activities

Non Cosmetic Participation

| Apolitical status | Commitment | Volunteering Intelligence |

Observation of rule of law

Reduction of Crime

Unity of purpose

Effective deployment

Establishment of bases/ posts

Social Responsibility

Improved Relaxations

...s approach to policing (Chingozha M.I.P. 2010)

115

While community policing is very promising in managing crime across societies, in Zimbabwe, there is evidence that many members of the public are reluctant to cooperate with the police. One question that immediately comes to mind is why?

Why many communities in Zimbabwe are reluctant to cooperate with police?

From the research we carried between 2010 and 2015 in Mashonaland West and Masvingo Provinces on police-public cooperation, a number of reasons were given as to why members of the public normally do not cooperate with the police in managing crime in their communities. The reasons which we received from both the members of the public and police include:

Reporting stations are usually away from the public
The public at times would fear being mugged again enroute to the police station. The majority of the police stations in the developing world were set up to protect the interests of their colonial masters thus they were positioned in a manner that made sure the interests of the master are secure.

Suggestion boxes are located at places that could jeopardise potential informants
As much as people might want to work hand in glove with the police they also fear for their lives. They fear being tracked by the criminals if they are seen placing tips into a suggestion box. Some have no confidence with the police to the extent that they feel bothered if called up to testify. They feel this could endanger them in the neighbourhood. Others

also feel that they would be inconvenienced if they were required to testify in a competent court of law while others still feel that the police are too interrogating.

Over-familiarisation of police officers and the public due to the fact that:

Police officers are, in the majority of cases, tenants because of the lack of accommodation in police camps. This compromises the officers a great deal because should they become overzealous yet they would not have any shelter or they would always be on the road relocating. They would be unpopular thus at times they are forced to pretend that what they are witnessing is not happening.

Lack of resources

The police officers also face many challenges with transport to and from work. Gone are the days when the state used to take care of the transport needs of its members in the third world. The police are having to deal with a depleted fleet. Coming from this background it would be very difficult then to effect an arrest on a traffic offender who could otherwise offer a free ride home. This is the dilemma and most officers are always at crossroads.

Poor remuneration

Governments in the third world countries like Zimbabwe are operating on very tight budgets which are making the operations and activities difficult for not only the police but the entire civil service.

The police and the people now have an appetite for corruption

It now goes without saying that the majority of citizens and members of the force have developed a cancer that may be difficult to remedy. People are now always keen to have the easy way out of problems. The people now have the appetite to offer and the appetite to receive. Corruption appears to be the in thing now, it is now fashionable, it is more like the norm.

Many police officers are no longer reliable

Many feel that it is no longer rewarding to be patient. Given the slightest opportunity the officers would want to reap as much as possible whatever it takes. It is rather saddening that the police are even said to be taking property from the deceased at scenes of accidents. This is confirmation that the morals of people have sunk to rock bottom. How honest can anyone do this without feeling guilty or being afraid of the dead, or are the dead no longer worth our respect and honour now?

Some police officers connive with accused persons

Saddening to note has been the development that the police are conniving with the accused to further prejudice the complainants. The police are said to be assisting the accused to get away with the crimes committed. They are no longer collecting sufficient evidence so that when the case is taken to court the evidence will be inadequate to secure a conviction. In some cases police officers have deliberately provided inadequate statements as a way of defeating the justice process.

Human rights violations by some members of the police

In some cases police officers assault or severely interrogate their suspects or accused persons in such a manner that it is viewed as an abuse by the victims and observers. In view of the contemporary policing initiatives being advocated for by most police services/forces no person should be belittled by a police officer in the course of his duties. All clients should be treated within the limits of the law. Whenever an accused person has been assaulted an offence would have been committed. In view of this, police officers are viewed as abusers of human rights and do not deserve any respect and cooperation. Police officers no longer comply with the ethics of policing a democratic state.

Appearances of police officers are no longer befitting
- They now smoke in public
- They eat food in public
- Seen carrying heavy luggage while in uniform
- Ignore attending scenes of crime because they will be in a rush to get home, to work or to do their own business

Some police officers no longer respect the interests and concerns of the lowly regarded in society
These usually do not have the capacity to reward the police officers in cash or kind. If the person does not offer something the police officer will not be motivated to assist. As a result, if at all they attend to these problems they do so half-heartedly.

Loss of public confidence in police
There is loss of public confidence because officers have now relegated their oath of office. In essence, they have intentionally dropped the critical responsibilities they are mandated to execute without question through the codification of social contract. Efforts to enhance the police public alliance are met with cynicism and scepticism because the public has been betrayed through the disregard of duty by police officers in the majority of cases.

Lack of customer care by some police officers

Some publics feel that police officers are rude in their dealings with them. Their sentiments are that the police officers particularly those on patrol and roadblocks feel that they are ultimate, invincible and can say or do anything to their victims yet they are supposed to be patient, tolerant and take time to explain any concerns raised by the supposed victims. The victims feel that they are reduced to boys and girls which belittle their humanity.

While the findings above are not universal in so far as only some members (whether of the public or police members) are involved, there is need to emphasise and promote good policing and relationship between the community and the police.

Ethical pill for good policing

As Dwivedi (1978) tells us, a problem of ethics in the public service may be said to exist whenever public servants, individually or collectively use positions in a way which compromises public confidence and trust because of conflicts of loyalties or as a result of attempts to achieve some form of private gain at the expense of public welfare or common good. And, as revealed in Dwivedi's observation, the problem of ethics normally culminates into vices such as corruption. Many scholars and institutions (e.g. World Bank 1997, 2000; Balboa and Medalla 2006) believe that while numerous conceptualisations of corruption have been advanced, all these definitions have a common denominator; that is, the use of public office with its paraphernalia of prestige, influence and power in order to make private gains which need not to be monetary, in breach of laws and regulations nominally in force.

According to Independent Corrupt Practices Commission (ICPC) Act section 2 of 2000, corruption includes vices like bribery, fraud and other related offences. The ICPC also sees corruption as the abuse of power or position of trust for personal or group benefit (monetary or otherwise). Similarly, corruption can be defined as 'the misuse or abuse of public office for private gains' (World Bank 1997, 2000; Balboa and Medalla 2006). This means that corruption can come in various forms and a wide array of illicit behaviour, such as bribery, extortion, fraud, nepotism, graft, speed money, pilferage, theft, and embezzlement, falsification of records, kickbacks, influence peddling, and campaign contributions (Klitgaard 1997). Important to note is the fact that while corruption is commonly attributed to the public sector, it also exists in other aspects of governance, such as political parties, private business sector, and NGO (USAID, Anti-corruption Strategy 2005). Further, the violation of established regulations during corrupt dealings is consistent with societally founded and supported patterns of behaviour and attitudes obtaining in all economies across the world. Tunde Agarah (1990) points out that whether developed or developing, no bureaucracy is free of corruption. With specific reference to Africa, Ekhomu defines bureaucratic corruption as:

[...] the direct or inadvertent thwarting of implementation process through either the accepting or asking for a bribe, suboptimal utilization of available resources due to selfish motivations and performance or non-performance of one's official duties with the view of achieving a private end which does not directly aggregate into community (Ekhomu cited in Makumbe 1998: 93-94).

Types of Unethical Conduct

➤ Bribes paid to have compromising documents removed from files or dockets.
➤ Fraudulent use of official stationery.
➤ Payment for letters of recommendation.
➤ Kickbacks for winning tenders.
➤ Misuse of official housing – such as taking in lodgers.
➤ Raising false claims.
➤ Threats.
➤ Unearned promotions.
➤ Unlawful detentions for a reward.

Factors that Influence Unethical Conduct

1. Socio-economic conditions.
-       high unemployment
-       widespread poverty
-       high inflation
-       low disposable income
-       low exchange rate (see also Makumbe 1998: 96).

2. Cultural factors – kinship loyalty
3. Nature of political system and its leadership
4. Ineffective ways of dealing with perpetrators
5. Lack of supervision

Unethical Behaviour in the Zimbabwe Republic Police

According to Makumbe (1998), in his paper presented at the Police Staff College, it was noted thatthe Zimbabwe Republic Police (ZRP) disclosed in October 1992 that the

Zimbabwe Government (ZG) had lost a total of Z$14,6 million (US$3 million) in the previous twelve months due to theft and fraud by public officials.

During the same period 26 cases of corruption were reportedin Government institutions in which more than $739 000 was received by some of the employees as bribes [...] (a total of) 350 cases of fraud had been reported. Cases of fraud and corruption were reported throughout the country and they involved junior and senior officers (Makumbe 1998: 97; also see Herald 6/10/1992).

The gravity of the matter is further underlined by the fact that some members of the police force are also involved in the depravity. At one time, virtually the whole top brass of the police force were undergoing trial for several unrelated charges. These included:

a). Acting Commissioner of Police – Contravening of the Prevention of Corruption Act (PCA);

b). Senior Assistant Commissioner – PCA – two charges plus charges of theft by conversion;

c). Senior Assistant Commissioner – Parks and Wildlife Act, plus attempt to defeat the course of justice;

d).Police Inspector – Parks and Wildlife plus attempt to defeat the course of justice;

e). Deputy Police Commissioner – Police Act, attempt to defeat the course of justice, Contempt.

This level of questionable behaviour among law enforcement agents the major custodians of law and order is a major indicator of the rapidity with which corruption is increasing in Zimbabwe. Indeed at the same time these police officers were undergoing trial, there were charges of fraud being levelled against the Attorney general (AG) himself. In

2008 the AG had to be arraigned before the courts for trial for perpetrating acts of unethical behaviour. He had to be relieved of his duties.

Possible solutions

The main problem with corruption and unethical conduct is that sometimes it is the senior officers themselves who are more corrupt and therefore anxious not to rock the boat in any way lest their misdemeanour be discovered. According to the Ombudsman's report cited by Makumbe (1998: 98):

Where supervision and accountability are non-existent publicofficers tend to carry out their duties with minimum regardto procedures, thereby exposing themselves to favouritismand partiality where this happens, corruption and abuse ofoffice have crept in.

The following are only suggestions for discussion since each of them will, obviously, generate its own administrative, financial and/or other problems.

- The ZRP should draw up a code of ethics for all its officers.
- Improve police officer's remuneration and other terms and conditions of service.
- Support of the Anti-Corruption Commission on a permanent basis to deal with cases of corruption among both the police and civilians.
- Campaigns in support of the concept of familyhood and communalism.
- Deterrent sentences on those who make offers to the police after committing crime.

- Operating above political party lines.
- Encouraging the judiciary to compliment the work of the police.
- Participating in regional workshops and seminars where notes are exchanged.
- Maintenance of resources available.
- Creating networks with various publics.
- The legal system in Zimbabwe should also be urged to impose severe sentences on convicted corrupt police officials than those imposed on civilian perpetrators.
- Further, convicted police officers should be made to compensate or reimburse society in real terms if it means selling their private property in order to do so.
- Besides, all police officers should sign a pledge of commitment to their nation and the service of the people without fear and favour. The following are suggestions of such a pledge:

-       I promise to act honestly and openly in all aspects of my life.

-       I will always put the welfare of the people of Zimbabwe ahead of my personal interests.

-       I pledge to be exemplary in my conduct of my duties in accordance with the laws of Zimbabwe without compromise.

-       I commit myself to fight unethical conduct among my colleagues in the ZRP and any other public officials in other institutions.

-       I pledge to uphold transparency in all that I do, individually or collectively, in the execution of my duties and responsibilities.

-        I promise to adopt a lifestyle which is consistent with my means and not to seek a lifestyle which I cannot afford to pay for, given my earning.

-        I commit myself to serve in such a way that I do not realise undue personal gain from the performance of my official duty.

-        I will avoid any interest or activity which is in conflict with the conduct of my official duties(Makumbe 1998: 98-99).

Corporate Governance

Comrade Dabengwa, the then Minister of Home Affairs, summed it well when he said that lack of transparency and accountability within the public service destroys the trust and confidence people have in their government and become a source of political instability (Towards Anti-Corruption Agency Seminar Report, 1999). This understanding is seconded by scholars like Janke (1998) who argues that the public give police enormous responsibilities and power to effectively discharge their duties; exceeding this authority, abusing the power and trust, make the public and the politicians nervous. All this betrays corporate governance. But what is corporate governance and why it is important?

Coyle (2003) refers to corporate governance as the way in which companies are governed, and to what purpose. It is concerned with practices and procedures for trying to ensure that a company is run in such a way that it achieves its objectives in an ethical way and in compliance with laws and regulations.

For Johnson and Scholes (1997), corporate governance generally include not only profit seeking companies but also non-profit ones by pointing out that, corporate governance involves the determination of minimum obligations of an organisation towards its various stakeholders. The determination of minimum obligations that Johnson and Scholes (1997) mean to ensure corporate governance is also applicable to the ZRP. As maintained by Johnson and Scholes such determination can only be realised if the organisation embraces key elements of corporate governance such as:

- Honesty
- Trust and integrity
- Openness
- Performance orientation
- Responsibility
- Mutual respect
- Commitment to the organisation
- Accountability

These key elements are enshrined in the five principles of corporate governance namely; leadership, capability, accountability, sustainability and integrity (Iwasaki 2013). Elaborating further on what each of the principles entail, Jo Iwasaki, explains that by leadership, we mean that an effective board should head each organisation to steer it [organisation] to meet its purpose in both the short and long term. Linked to this principle is capability, which for Iwasaki, entails the board's appropriate mix of skills, experience and independence that enable its members to discharge responsibilities and duties effectively. These two principles are also linked to accountability, that is, the board's obligation to communicate to the organisation's shareholders and other stakeholders, at regular intervals, a fair, balanced and understandable assessment of how the organisation is achieving its objectives. On the principle of sustainability, Iwasaki, explains that this is the principle that guides the organisation to create value and allocate it fairly and appropriately to all stakeholders. Onintegrity, Iwasaki explains that this is the principle that allows the board of an organisation to conduct its activities in a fair and transparent manner that can withstand scrutiny by stakeholders.

As could be seen from the elaborations above, each of the five principles articulated above cannot work in isolation. The principles are closely related such that failure to recognise any one of them compromises the performance of an organisation.

Attitude of Commissioner General of Police (CGP) to corporate governance

He is quoted in his radio message AC 01/2005 to all stations in Zimbabwe dated 16th February 2005 in which he said:

> Officers must be reminded individually and severally that they joined the police to work and serve, and that to that effect they have sworn. Complaints reaching this office from several parts of the country speak volumes of laziness, lack of diligence, lack of commitment to duty, illegal arrests and detentions, asking for bribes on the roads and several other acts of misbehaviour and mischief to total criminality. Reports of theft of government property from camps have also been noted and this is obviously an internal job. This office calls upon individuals within the organisation to be obedient, to be courteous, to work hard, to be committed and to fulfil the purpose each individual madeon joining the force so that our service delivery is improved [...] The entire and full command,

this office inclusive, is set to monitor this trend, which has to be halted.

The speech by the Commissioner General of Police in Zimbabwe invokes a mind boggling question that both members of the public and those of the police force in the country should grapple with all the time. The question is: 'What makes a police officer a good police?' Before we respond to this question we want to stress that the question does not beg for a one word answer. This means the question is complex in a way though the answer could be summarised as below: A good police force is one that is committed to the ideals of the social contract. It has to completely address the obligations it stands for.

The facets of a good police include:
- Commitment to upholding the national constitution,
- Commitment to upholding democratic values,
- Dealing with crime prevention,
- Upholding the sanctity of life,
- Involving neighbourhood in policing,
- Involvement in social responsibility,
- Operating in a responsible and transparent manner,
- Making all officers accountable for their actions so that they will not be overzealous in pursuit of selfish ends,
- Avoiding underhand dealings or palm greasing (integrity),
- Non-militaristic.

In short, all police officers ought to be properly socialised so that these values are cultivated in them. These are the values that are the cornerstone to the success of a positive police force. Upholding these values will persuade the public

129

to come into an enduring alliance with the police. They will be convinced that it is a people's force, and not a group of insensitive, corrupt and incompetent lot.

A good police is the one that looks beyond the station of someone in life in the management of crime. It looks at all people as being equal before the law and requiring the same protection if violated in whatever form. This is because a good police force is characterised by self-directed and fired up officers whose vision is to see a reduced crime rate in the rate in the area of policing. The officers should feel a burden within their inner persons to deal with crime.

Framework for good governance in the ZRP

Just like many other institutions, the Zimbabwe Republic Police (ZRP), does not operate in a vacuum, but in a society with people. This being the case, the ZRP is guided by principles, a framework for good governance, in all its operations. These include:

Service Charter

The Service Charter promises to the public efficiency, effectiveness, professionalism, accountability, transparency, diligence, courtesy, honesty and integrity, all of which constitute the hallmark of good governance.

Section B of the Police Act
The CGP is required by Section 13 of the Police Act to submit an annual report to the Minister of Home Affairs. This report is then tabled in parliament. This report details:

-   activities of the police during the year

- policy directives given to him by the Minister
- reports on results of investigation of any cases which may have been referred to him by the AG for investigation.

Code of Conduct

The Zimbabwe Republic Police has a code of conduct for both the senior management and the junior members.Sections 29 and 34 of the Police Act, for example, provide for a schedule of offences which are meant to regulate the conduct of officers and members in the conduct of their police business.

Now that we have put to the open the code of conduct and enunciated the Service Charter for police officers, there is need to look at the role of police in a changing society or what we call society in transition.

The role of the police in preserving peace and order in a changing society

The environment is constantly changing as a result of various developments in the dynamism and turbulence prevailing. These changes which in the majority of cases are inevitable demand that institutions change or adapt so that they do not trail or lag behind such new developments. The developments at times come so fast and with so much impact.

No focused management can afford to ignore change when it descends. Change is triggered by a plethora of change drivers that include:

- Economic changes
- Technological factors
- Legal – politico changes

131

- Ecological developments
- Socio-cultural changes
- Globalisation

The police force, thus, is expected to assume a number of roles in a changing society, chief of which are:

Protection of society

The police force is not an exception in responding to change because as times evolve the role of the police also shifts from one dimension to another. It [the police force] has to be responsive to such changes as they are experienced so that the police force remains relevant in pursuit of the constitutional mandate as defined in Section 93 (1) of the Constitution of Zimbabwe. This section details:

> For the purpose of preserving the internal security of and maintaining law and order in Zimbabwe there shall be a police force and every member of that force is charged with the general duty of maintaining law and order, of taking all steps which on reasonable grounds appear to him to be necessary for preserving peace, for protecting property from malicious injury, for the detection of crime and for apprehending offenders and suppressing all forms of civil commotion or disturbance that may occur in any part of Zimbabwe.

In a nutshell, the constitution gives the police a mandate to ensure social peace, free and unimpeded enjoyment of the various liberties prescribed by this provision. The various challenges, developments within and without the country can instigate unfriendly changes which might cause the police to change course, to redesign their operations, reconfigure their networks, rethink their ways and re-launch their missiles for results.

As societies move from one level of development to another the thinking of the people also changes. In this vein the people in Zimbabwe are more aware of their rights unlike in the yesteryear when they were policed by the lethal colonial force which perpetuated the interests of the minority whites. The people of Zimbabwe are now aware of the provisions of Section 11 of the Constitution of Zimbabwe which provides for the 'prohibition of discrimination in whatever form, to live freely, to be protected by the law, liberty, security, protection of private property from compulsory acquisition without compensation.'

Given that changes are occurring everywhere, there is no point in clinging to old ways of doing things. Makumbe (1998) in a paper presented to the ZRP Staff College quoted the Attorney General, the Honourable P. A. Chinamasa who at the seminar for senior CID officers at Troutbeck Inn, Nyanga made the following comments:

> In your efforts to improve and attain higher and even higher levels of efficiency, you will find that your biggest obstacle to progress is inertia. It is easy to forsake old ways of thinking and doing things. The tendency always is not to want to think how differently we can do things we have been doing over the years. The tendency always is not to ask why we continue doing them and whether doing them still serves a purpose... There is no reason why change should be resisted.

It is important to acknowledge that before any change process can be considered there should be organized consultation especially with the people who would be involved in the implementation of the change. The need for change must also start from the top as can be seen from the foreword by the Commissioner of Police, Augustine Chihuri, to Focus 200 Strategic Planning where he is quoted as having said:

The Zimbabwe Republic Police is aiming at improving co-operations, so that it may provide the best possible service to the public. The aim is seen against the back drop of increasing and shifting public demands and finite resources calls for meticulous planning for it to be realised.

As a partner in crime management

The consciousness that the people now have would not allow them to be abused, taken advantage of by any one even the police force. They would voice hence the need to be a people's force that operates within the framework that is people oriented. What this means is that the people and the police should have a good working relationship. Gone are the years when the police was viewed as a monster. Today's thinking is that the police are an equal partner in the fight against crime so that the community is habitable. Such rapport would also guarantee the effective and timely flow of relevant information from the public to the police to ensure that criminals are accounted for.

As a source of information

The police force is expected by the people to be a reservoir of information. The people will always expect the police to be knowledgeable about whatever issue that the people bring to their attention. This could range from:

- How to locate a particular street in town
- The current political developments

- The location of the welfare offices
- Government policies
- Animal diseases, firewood etc.

Competent first aiders

The public always takes relief on the sight of a police officer where an incident or accident has occurred. He must acquit himself well in this regard as well as the management of the traffic accident scene. The public is not aware of police departments. It would not be good enough for one to say he cannot deal with a scene of accident because he is not a traffic officer, or because he is in the support services of the force. The police officer is thus expected to be versatile, he must rise and equal any task in as far as preserving loss of life is concerned.

Conflict resolution

Wherever the police officer is, he will be expected to be in a position to preside over any form of conflict and to meaningfully contribute towards its resolution. The officer is thus expected to be knowledgeable about a host of subjects so as to contribute meaningfully in the resolution of conflicts lest he becomes a disgrace. The officer should always prevail over those coming to him for assistance. In this vein the officer is expected to be well resourced with information that is handy.

Being a role model

As a disciplined force that it is, its members are expected to inspire those around them. They are expected to be role models, members of society who are beyond reproach, upright and exemplary. They will be an example to the youths in their locality which will be a step towards a crime free community. This is the thrust of the Home Officers Scheme and the junior call. When youths admire the police, they will not contemplate engaging in criminal activities.

Adaptive professional

Crime trends are always changing. The police force is expected to be wary of the recent developments and technologies so that they come up with strategies that are relevant in the circumstances. This is particularly so in view of economic crimes. The police force has always trailed the criminals. The hackers are always a step ahead in view of cybercrimes but the people still expect the police to expeditiously work out strategies to deal with the challenges before much prejudice on the unsuspecting public. Resources must always be availed in a bid to be swift in dealing with new crimes.

Reputable and non-partisan

The police force should be in a position to contain situations. It should not be too politicized, that is too close to the government of the day. The impact of too close a relationship between these two would tend to cause it to lose the respect and support of any part of the population tending to disagree with the government on any issue. A police force ought to be independent. The police must also uphold the rule of law by use of minimum force with respect for human rights. The police force must not be associated with any one population group to avoid the growth of the "us and them" attitude in the minds of the group excluded from participation in police activities. In other words in a changing society the police must be seen to be independent but vigorous in its activities, non-discriminatory, completely open and incorrupt.

Responsible and accountable figure

The police force deals with members of the public all day in various engagements. Some come as complainants, witnesses, informants and accused or suspects. All these individuals look up to the police to act responsibly in their different circumstances. The police are not expected to abuse the so much power vested in them. This explains what Lord Acton meant when he said: 'Power tends to corrupt, and absolute power corrupts absolutely. Great men are almost always bad men. There is no worse heresy than the office sanctifies the holder of it'.In response to this Judge Gillespie said,

> The way it corrupts is by breeding first pride. Understandable human pride in achievement or position can quickly become arrogance. Arrogance can quickly breed a belief in one's unaccountability that is the temptation to wrongdoing. It is human nature. Judges are not immune to it. Police are not immune to it. No human is. Fight against pride. See yourselves as servants. Then your power might not corrupt you.

While addressing senior police officers in 1997 at the Police Staff College on 'The role of police in a changing society,' Judge Gillespie furthered to say:

> It is in his dealings with criminals and suspects that a police officer will always believe that his suspicion is right yet it might not in some circumstances. This in many times forces the police officer to fabricate evidence or exaggerate facts to secure a conviction. This is not expected in a dynamic and democratic society which seeks to uphold human rights. The police will not be doing any just when they bully, torture or give false evidence in a competent court of law. A man must

137

be convicted in view of overwhelming evidence not on his own confessions because of having been threatened, beaten, and abused by the police.

The police should also rise above political party lines. It should treat all citizens alike. No citizen is indispensable or above the law. The law of the land should be applied uniformly and consistently to all citizens if the police force is to earn a modicum of respect from within and without the country.

References

Agarah, T. 1990. Check and balances of bureaucratic excesses and corruption in Nigeria: An assessment of the Public Complaints Commission, *African Administrative Studies*, No. 35: 27-44.

Alderson J. 1998. *Principled Policing: Protecting the Public with Integrity*, Waterside Press, Winchester.

Amnesty International, AFR 46/003/2005.

Annan, K. 2002. *United Nations Millennium Campaign*, End Poverty, United Nations.

Appiahene-Gyamfi, J. 2003. Urban crime trends and patterns in Ghana: The case of Accra, *Journal of Criminal Justice*, 31 (1): 13-23.

Aquinas, T. 'The essence of law', in Pegis, A.C. (Ed). 1948. *Introduction to St Thomas Aquinas*, Random House: New York.

Austin, J. 1832. *The province of jurisprudence determined*, Weidenfeld and Nicolson, London.

Balboa, J. and Medalla, E. M. 2006. Anti-corruption and governance: The Philippine experience, *Philippine APEC Study Centre Network*, Ho Chi Minh City: Viet Nam.

Baker, B. 2008. Beyond the tarmac road: Local forms of policing in Sierra Leone and Rwanda, *Review of African Political Economy* 35 (118):555-70.

Baker, B. 2008b. *Multi-choice policing in Africa*, Nordiska Afrika Institute, UPPSALA.

Baker, B. 2002a. Living with non-state policing in South Africa: The issues and dilemmas, *Journal of Modern African Studies*, 40 (1): 29-53.

Baker, B. 2002b. *Taking the law into their own hands*, Ashgate: Aldershot.

Bastin, Y., Coupez, A., Mann, M. 1999. Continuity and divergence in the Bantu languages: Perspectives from a lexicostatistic study, *Annales Sciences Humanines* 162: 313-317.

Bayart, J. S. *et al.* 1999. *The criminalisation of the state in Africa*, James Currey: Oxford.

Bayley, D. and Shearing, C. 2001. *The new structure of policing: Description, conceptualisation and research agenda,* US Department of Justice, National Institute of Justice, Washington DC.

Buttner, E. 1974. *Florence Nightingale in pursuit of Willie Sutton: A theory of the police*, Sage Publishers: London.

Byers, B. 2002. Ethics and criminal justice: Some observations on police misconduct, *Crime and Justice International,* Vol. 18- Issue 68.

Chapman, B. 1970. *Police State*, Pall Mall Press Ltd: London.

Chaza, A.G. 1998. *Bhurakuwacha: Black policeman in Rhodesia*, College Press: Harare.

Chevallier, G. 1936. *Penguin No. 797: Clochemerle*, Penguin Books, London.

Clapman, C. 1999. African security systems: Privatisation and the scope for Mercenary activity, In Mills, G. and Stremlau, J. (Eds). *The privatisation of security in Africa*, South African Institute of International Affairs, 23-24.

Chukwuma, I. 2001. Police transformation in Nigeria: Problems and prospects, *Paper presented at Crime and Policing in Transitional Societies Conference*, August 30- September 1 2000, South Africa. Available at: www.kas.de/proj/home.

Cohn, W. A. 1978. *The future of policing*, Alibris: United States of America.

Collins Concise Dictionary, 1988. United Kingdom.

Constitution of Zimbabwe Amendment (No. 20) Act 2013.

Crawshaw, R. 1999. *Police and Human Rights: A manual for Teachers, Resource Persons and Participants in Human Rights Programmes*, Kluwer Law International, Netherlands.

Criminal Justice, 1995. *Aims and objectives*, Scottish Executive Consultations: Scotland.

Critchley, T. A. 1967. *A history of police in England and Wales*, Constable: London.

Dalgleish, D. 2005. Pre-colonial criminal justice in West Africa: Eurocentric thought versus Africentric evidence, *African Journal of Criminology and Justice Studies*, 1 (1): 55-69.

Davey, B. J. 1983. *Lawless and immoral: Policing a country Town 1838-1857*, Leicester University Press: Leicester.

DeGeorge, R. T. 1982. *Ethics and business*, Macmillan Publishing Company, London.

Dinsmor, A. 2003. *Glasgow Police Pioneers*, The Scotia News (Winter 2003), Scotland.

Diop, C. A. 1987. *Pre-colonial Black Africa*, Lawrence Hill Books, New York.

Dwivendi, P. O. 1978. Public service ethics, *International Review of Administrative Sciences*, 1-10.

Ebbe, O. N. I. (Ed). 2000. *Comparative and international criminal justice systems: Policing, judiciary and corrections*, Butterworth-Heinemann: Boston.

Edwards, P. 1996. *The encyclopaedia of philosophy*, Vol. 3 and 4, Macmillan: New York.

Ehret, C. 2001. *An African Classical Age*, University Press of Virginia.

Emsley, C. 1996. (2nd ed.) *Crime and society in England 1750-1900*, Longman, London and New York.

Farringdon, K. 1996. *History of punishment and torture*, Chancellor Press: London.

Feltoe, G. 1998. 'Planning and human rights', In Schlicht, M. *Policing in a democratic society*, Occasional Papers, Harare: Zimbabwe.

Findlay, J. N. 1993. *Plato: The written and unwritten doctrines*, Routledge and Kegan Paul Ltd.

Frey, L. and Frey, M. 2004. *The French Revolution*, Greenhood Press: Connecticut.

Furet, F. 1995. *Revolutionary France 1770-1800*, Blackwell Publishing.

Gabriel, C. and Scott, W. 1998. The Blue Wall of Silence 'as evidence of bias and motive to lie': A new approach to police perjury, *University of Pittsburgh Law Review 59*: 233-296.

Ghanaian Chronicle (28 July 2003), Accra: Ghana.

Gibbs, P. Et al. 1981. *Blue and old gold: The history of the British South Africa Police 1889-1980*, Out of Print Books.

Grant, J. 2003. Assault under colour of authority: Police corruption as norm in the LAPD Rampart Scandal and in Popular Film, *New Political Science 25* (3): 404.

Graeber, D. 2001. *Towards an Anthropological Theory of Value: The False Coin of Our Own Dreams*, Palgrave: New York.

Guthrie, M. 1967. *Comparative Bantu: An introduction to the comparative linguistics and pre-history of the Bantu languages*, Gregg International.

Hahlo, H. R. and Kahn, E. 1968. *The South African legal system and its background*, Juta and Company: Cape Town, South Africa.

Hall, M., Stephen, W., Silliman, S. 2005. *Historical Archaeology*, Wiley Blackwell.

Harlan, H. 1971. *Police in Urban Society*, Sage Publications: California

Harper, T. (10 Jan 2014). 'Exclusive Scotland Yard's rotten core: Police failed to address Met's endemic corruption-crime', *The IndependentNewspaper*, UK.

Hart, H. L. A. 1961. *The Concept of Law*, Oxford University Press: Oxford.

Hegel, G. 1956. *The Philosophy of History*, Dover: New York.

Hills, A. 2000. *Policing in Africa: Internal security and the limits of liberalisation*, Lynne Rienner: Boulder.

Holden, C. J. 2002. Bantu language trees reflect the spread of farming across sub-Saharan Africa, *Proc. R. Soc.* London: 793-799.

Huffman, T. N. 2007. *Handbook to the Iron Age*, University of KwaZulu-Natal, South Africa.

Humphries, R. 2000. *Crime and Confidence: Voters' perceptions of crime*, Needlebank ISS Crime Index 4 (2): 1-6.

Hunt, L. 1984. Politics, culture and class in the French Revolution, University of California Press: Berkeley.

Hunwick, J. O. 1999. *Timbuktu and the Songhai Empire: Al-Sadi's Tarikh al-Sudan down to 1613 and other contemporary documents*, Brill: Netherlands.

Ingram, D. 2006. Law: *Key concepts in philosophy*, Continuum: London.

Independent Corrupt Practices Commission (ICPC) Act section 2 of 2000, Harare: Zimbabwe.

Ivkovic, K. S. 2003. To serve and collect: Measuring police corruption, *The Journal of Criminal Law and Criminology 93*, No: 2/3: 600.

Iwasaki, J. (18 Nov. 2013). What are the overarching principles of corporate governance? *Paper Presented to ICAEW*, New Statesman Blog.

Johnston, L. 2000. *Policing Britain: Risk, security and governance*, Harlow: Longman, England.

Johnston, L. 2002. The transformation of policing? Understanding current trends in policing systems, *British Journal of Criminology* 42, 129-46.

Johnston, L. 1996. Policing diversity: The impact of the public-private complex in policing, in Leishman, F., Loveday, B. and Savage, S. (Eds). *Core issues in policing* (Vol. 1), Longman, London, pp. 54-74.

Johnston, L. and Shearing, C. 2003. *Governing security*, Routledge: London.

Kammer, C. L. 1988. *Ethics and liberation: An introduction*, S.C.M. Press Ltd: London.

Kati, M. 1913. (republished 1981). *Tarikh el-Fettach (History for the truth seeker;* trans into French by Houdas, O. And Delafosse, M. A. Maisonneuve: Paris.

Kempa, M. et al. 2004. Policing communal spaces: A reconfiguration of the 'Mass Private Property' hypothesis, *British Journal of Criminology* (2004) 44, 562-581.

Killingray, D. 1997. Securing the British Empire: Policing and colonial order, 1920-1960, in Killingray, D. 1986.The maintenance of law and order in British colonial Africa, *African Affairs*, 85: 411-437.

Klitgaard, R. 1997. "Strategies against Corruption", Available at: http://www.clad.org.ve/klit3.htm.p.1. (Accessed 15 May 2012).

Kratcoski, P. 2002. International perspectives on institutional and police corruption, *Police Practice and Research 3* (1): 74-79.

Levtzion, N. And Spaulding, J. (Eds). *Medieval West Africa: Views from Arab scholars and Merchants*, Markus Wiener Publishers: Princeton.

Loader, I. 2000. Plural policing and democratic governance, *Social and Legal Studies* 9 (3): 323-45.

Longman Contemporary English Dictionary, 2007. Longman, London.

Lugard, L. 1996. *A tropical dependency*, James Nisbet and Co: UK.

Mackey, T. 1997. 'Meat-eaters and grass-eaters', in H-Net, November 1997. Available at: http://www.h-net.org/reviews/showrev.php?id=1503.

Madhuku, L. 2010. *An introduction to Zimbabwean law*, Weaver Press, Harare: Zimbabwe.

Makumbe, M. W. J. 1998. Police ethics in theory and practice-paper 11, Management Development Seminars (July/August 1995), in *Policing in a democratic society*, Occasional Papers, Harare: Zimbabwe.

Mawere, M. 2011. *Moral degeneration in contemporary Zimbabwean business practices*, Langaa RPCIG: Bamenda.

Mawere, M. *etal*. 2012. *Memoirs of an unsung legend*, Langaa RPCIG: Bamenda.

Mayhall, P. 1985. *Police-community relations and the administration of justice*, 3rd ed, John Wiley and Sons, New York.

Mazower, M. ed. *The policing of politics in the twentieth century*, Providence and Oxford: Berghahn Books, 167-190.

McCracken, G. 1986. Culture and consumption: A theoretical account of the structure and movement of the cultural meaning of consumer goods, *Journal of Consumer Research* 13 (June): 71-84.

Mcketta, F. 2000. *Police, politics, corruption: The mixture dangerous to freedom and justice*, MClain Printing Company: West Virginia.

Mitchell, P. Whitelaw, G. 2005. The archaeology of southernmost Africa from c.2000Bp to the early 1800s: A review of recent research, *Journal of African History 46*: 209-241.

Mullen, A. (8 Nov. 2011). 'Breaching the Blue Code,' *Metro Times Newspaper*, London.

Murphy, J. G. And Coleman, J. L. 1984. *The philosophy of law: An introduction*, Rowman and Littlefield Publishers: New Jersey.

Newburn, T. 1999. Understanding and preventing police corruption: Lessons from the literature, *Police Research Series*, Paper 110, 1999.

Nyamnjoh, F.B. 2015. *C'est l'homme qui fait l'homme: Cul-de-Sac Ubuntu-ism in Côte d'Ivoire*, Langaa RPCIG: Bamenda.

Ollorwi, O. 2013. *Community policing and crime control in pre-colonial Eleme: Issues and perspectives*, Nigerian Institute of Security Studies, Port Harcourt: Nigeria.

O'Malley, P. 1997. Policing, politics, post-modernity, *Social and Legal Studies*, 6 (3): 363-81.

Onwudiwe, I. 2000. Decentralisation of the Nigerian Police Force, *The International Journal of African Studies* 2 (1): 95-114.

Paul, H. 2007. *The A to Z of the French Revolution*, Scarecrow Press: London.

Peng, W. 2013. The rise of the Red Mafia in China: A case study of organised crime and corruption in Chongqing, *Trends in Organised Crime 16* (1): 49-73.

Phillipson, D. W. 1989. Bantu-speaking people in southern Africa, in Obenga (ed). *Les Peuples Bantu*, Paris.

Policy Studies Institutions, (n.d.). The role and responsibility of the police, *Police Studies Institute*, Scotland.

Policing Studies Institute, (n.d). *The role and responsibility of the police*, United Kingdom.

Popkin, R. and Stroll, A. 1972. *Introduction to philosophy*, 2nd ed. Holt and Winston, New York.

Rexova, K., Bastin, Y., Frynta, D. 2006. Classic analysis of Bantu languages, *Naturwissenschften*. Doi:10.1007/s00114-006-0088-2.

Rowe, M. 2007. (1st Edn). *Introduction to policing*, Sage Publishers, London.

Said, E. 1993. *Culture and imperialism*, Chatto and Windus, London.

Schmolka, V. (n.d). Principles to guide criminal law reform, *Department of Justice*, Government of Canada.

Shaw, W. 1991. *Business ethics*, Macmillan Publishing Company, London.

Shearing, C. and Kempa, M. 2000. The role of private security in transitional democracies, *A paper presented at Crime and Policing in Transitional Societies Conference*, August 30-September 1, 2000, South Africa.

Skolnick, J. 2002. Corruption and the Blue Code of Silence, *Police Practice and Research 3* (1): 8-19.

Steadman, C. 1998. *Policing the Victorian Community: The formation of English Provincial forces*, Routledge and Kegan Paul: London.

Storch, R. 1975. The plague of Blue locusts: Police reform and popular resistance in northern England 1840-1857, International Review of Social History 20: 61-90.

The Global Fund. 2005. *Country statistics and disease indicators: Statistical yearbook*, Washington DC:USA.

The Herald Newspaper, 6 October 1992.

The Military Balance, 2003/2004. International Institute for Strategic Studies.

The Times of Zambia, Ndola 24 July 2003, Zambia.

Thurman, Q. and Giacomazzi, A. 2010. *Controversies in policing*, Elsevier, USA.

Trojanowicz, R. C. and Bucqueroux, B. 1994.*Community policing: How to get started*, Cincinnati OH: Anderson.

Trojanowicz, R. C. and Dixon, S. L. 1974. *Criminal justice and the community*, Englewood Cliffs: New Jersey.

Walker, S. 1992. Origins of the contemporary criminal justice paradigm: The American Bar Foundation Survey, 1953-1969, *Justice Quarterly 9* (1): 47-76.

Walker, R. and Millar, S. 2000. *Sword, Seal and Koran: The glorious West African empire of Songhai (c. 250 BC – 1660 AD)*, Concept learning: Birmingham.

World Bank, 2000. Anti-corruption policies programmes: A framework for evaluation, *Policy Research Working Paper 2501*, World Bank, Washington DC.

UN-HABITAT, 2001. *Crime in Nairobi-Results of a victim survey*, Nairobi: Kenya.

UN-HABITAT. 2003. *Global reports on human settlements 2003: The challenge of slums*, Nairobi: Kenya.

USAID. 2005. *USAID Anti-corruption strategy*. Retrieved April 05, 2013. Available at: http://www.usaid.gov/our_work/democracy_and_g overnance/publications/pdfs/ac_st rategy_final.pdf.

Young, C. 1994. *African colonial state in comparative perspective*, Yale University Press.

Zimbabwe Broadcasting Corporation (ZBC) News, *ZRP re-launches service charter*, Saturday 12 April 2014, Harare: Zimbabwe.